YORK NOTES

The Taming of the Shrew

William Shakespeare

Note by Rebecca Warren

 Longman

York Press

Exterior picture of the Globe Theatre reproduced by permission of the Raymond Mander and Joe Mitchenson Theatre Collection
Reconstruction of the Globe Theatre interior reprinted from Hodges: *The Globe Restored* (1968) by permission of Oxford University Press

Rebecca Warren is hereby identified as author of this work in accordance with Section 77 of the Copyright, Designs and Patents Act 1988

YORK PRESS
322 Old Brompton Road, London SW5 9JH

PEARSON EDUCATION LIMITED
Edinburgh Gate, Harlow,
Essex CM20 2JE, United Kingdom
Associated companies, branches and representatives throughout the world

First published 2000
Fifth impression 2002

ISBN 0-582-42460-7

Designed by Vicki Pacey
Phototypeset by Gem Graphics, Trenance, Mawgan Porth, Cornwall
Colour reproduction and film output by Spectrum Colour
Produced by Pearson Education North Asia Limited, Hong Kong

CONTENTS

PART ONE

INTRODUCTION

How to Study a Play 5
Reading *The Taming of the Shrew* 6

PART TWO

SUMMARIES & COMMENTARIES

Note on the Text 8
Synopsis 8
Detailed Summaries 10
- Induction 10
- Act I 14
- Act II 21
- Act III 28
- Act IV 34
- Act V 43

PART THREE

CRITICAL APPROACHES

Characterisation 49
- Petruchio 49
- Katherina 52
- Bianca 54
- Baptista 55
- The Suitors: Lucentio, Hortensio, Gremio 56
- The Servants 57
- Christopher Sly 58

Themes 59
- Romance & Marriage 59
- Money & Society 62
- Deception 62

Imagery 64
- The Devil 64
- Animals, Hunting & Hawking 65

Education 67
Food & Clothing 68
Language & Style 70
Structure 73

Part four

Textual analysis
Text 1 77
Text 2 81
Text 3 86

Part five

Background
William Shakespeare's Life 90
Shakespeare's Dramatic Career 91
The Texts of Shakespeare's Plays 92
Shakespeare & the English Renaissance 93
Shakespeare's Theatre 96
Reading Shakespeare 100

Part six

Critical history & broader perspectives
The Play in Performance 103
Early Views 103
Twentieth-Century Views 105
Current Approaches 107

Chronology 112
Literary Terms 114
Author of this Note 117

PART ONE

INTRODUCTION

HOW TO STUDY A PLAY

Studying on your own requires self-discipline and a carefully thought-out work plan in order to be effective.

- Drama is a special kind of writing (the technical term is 'genre') because it needs a performance in the theatre to arrive at a full interpretation of its meaning. Try to imagine that you are a member of the audience when reading the play. Think about how it could be presented on the stage, not just about the words on the page.
- Drama is always about conflict of some sort (which may be below the surface). Identify the conflicts in the play and you will be close to identifying the large ideas or themes which bind all the parts together.
- Make careful notes on themes, character, plot and any subplots of the play.
- Why do you like or dislike the characters in the play? How do your feelings towards them develop and change?
- Playwrights find nonrealistic ways of allowing an audience to see into the minds and motives of their characters, for example **soliloquy**, **aside** or music. Consider how such dramatic devices are used in the play you are studying.
- Think of the playwright writing the play. Why were these particular arrangements of events, characters and speeches chosen?
- Cite exact sources for all quotations, whether from the text itself or from critical commentaries. Wherever possible find your own examples from the play to back up your opinions.
- Always express your ideas in your own words.

This York Note offers an introduction to *The Taming of the Shrew* and cannot substitute for close reading of the text and the study of secondary sources.

This play has attracted so much opprobrium during the past hundred years, including calls to have it removed from the theatrical repertoire, that it is difficult to know whether to begin this Note with an apology for or defence of *The Shrew*. Perhaps – since the ideas and actions it contains arouse such strong feelings – no apology is necessary for this **comedy**. While audiences, readers and critics find something to argue about, surely Shakespeare's version of a traditional wife-taming story is worth watching and discussing?

What has caused the controversy? The final sentence of the previous paragraph encapsulates the problem: this is a play in which a woman is starved into submission. Her husband, seen by some as a lively scamp and by others as a brutal scoundrel, employs a range of stratagems to curb his bride's headstrong humour: he deprives her of sleep, bombards her with lectures about wifely obedience, denies her clothes and kisses until she finally acts in a way that pleases him. Depending upon your point of view, the heroine is either taught how to behave in a manner befitting her sex and station in life, or forced to submit to a domestic tyrant. No wonder critics as illustrious as George Bernard Shaw have decided *The Shrew* is unfit for the stage. The events outlined above are doubtless objectionable to many modern readers and theatregoers. And yet *The Taming of the Shrew* continues to interest and absorb us.

Why does the play remain so stubbornly popular? Why have there been so many successful adaptations, including the Cole Porter musical, *Kiss Me Kate*? The answer lies in the text's wit and exuberance. There are interludes of highly entertaining visual comedy. A modern audience often finds itself trapped in a curious position, rather like the heroine. While abhorring the sentiments of a drama that seems to advocate wife-taming as a prerequisite for a harmonious marriage, we find ourselves engaged by what is happening on stage. As well as being a rascal, Petruchio, the protagonist, is quick-witted, confident and funny: he is above all a wonderfully imaginative actor. His breathless wooing and wedding of the headstrong scold are theatrically compelling. And the minor characters are excellent comic foils, from Grumio, Petruchio's complaining manservant, to Tranio, the wily deceiver, who disguises himself in order to help his master Lucentio win the hand of fair Bianca. Added to the two fast-moving plots, which both focus on marriage, there is an entertaining and intriguing **Induction**, which frames the action of the play. This is the only Induction in Shakespeare's drama, and it is a masterly example of the form, with another fine comic character in the shape of Christopher Sly, the Warwickshire tinker. The action in the Sly Induction foreshadows the events of both plot and subplot. The whole play is full of amusing intrigues and deceptions, and the word-play is swift and hilarious. With the exception of Kate, the characters in *The Shrew* are having the time of their lives. And it is possible to argue that even Katherina learns that she will enjoy life more if she joins in with the game.

Shakespeare's tale of wife-taming was inspired by ballads, plays and folklore. It is part of a large body of literature dealing with the age-old war between the sexes, one of the stories most commonly reworked in every age. As such, it deserves attention. *The Taming of the Shrew* is also worth studying because it is an early comedy, and we see here some of the ideas that will preoccupy the dramatist in later works: the problematical relationships between parents and children and men and women, and the difficulty of negotiating appearances and reality. In *The Shrew* we see Shakespeare exploring the nature of romance and marriage, which he continued to do many times in subsequent plays. In particular, the playwright's evocation of the shrewish scold is intriguing, and troubling. This is his only drama in which a woman is severely punished for speaking her mind; later heroines are allowed to speak for and defend themselves. Kate is an interesting anomaly. By the time Shakespeare came to write *Much Ado About Nothing* (*c.* 1598), the professed man-hater Beatrice is allowed to get away with a great many more jibes against the opposite sex, while still being presented as an attractive and desirable partner. The message of this play, that domestic harmony depends upon breaking a woman's spirit, or at least on marrying a quiet, obedient female, is not repeated elsewhere. Hero, the silent heroine in *Much Ado*, will suffer greatly; in this comedy, the seemingly submissive and modest Bianca reveals herself as a shrew. Perhaps, then, there are two messages to be taken from *The Shrew*: the second, that women will have their own way somehow, when it is least expected!

PART TWO

SUMMARIES & COMMENTARIES

The history of the text we study and watch performed on stage today is complex, and its authorship has been the subject of dispute. Like Shakespeare's other plays, The Taming of the Shrew *was not published during the playwright's lifetime. Another play, sometimes thought to be an imperfect reconstruction or early version of* The Shrew *was published in 1594.* The Taming of A Shrew *shares the taming plot and romantic subplot with* The Shrew, *and Sly is present in both texts. The husbands' taming methods are similar, and occasionally there are verbal echoes of one text in the other play. It has been suggested that* A Shrew *should be regarded as a source for Shakespeare's drama (other sources are discussed in Language & Structure).*

The first version of The Shrew *appeared in the First Folio, a collection of Shakespeare's plays published in 1623, seven years after the playwright's death. Modern editions of the text are based on this version, which is thought to have been taken from a manuscript, most likely a transcript or draft of Shakespeare's. It is difficult, however, to arrive at a date of composition or first performance for* The Shrew. *Some commentators argue that this early comedy is less sophisticated than* A Comedy of Errors *and must predate it (the date of this play is also contentious); others prefer to believe that* The Shrew *came later. The text's relationship to* A Shrew *adds to the difficulty. Brian Morris, editor of the Arden edition used in the preparation of this Note – William Shakespeare,* The Taming of the Shrew, *ed., Brian Morris, The Arden Shakespeare, Routledge, 1981 – argues that the play must have been written earlier than August 1592.*

SYNOPSIS

Returning from hunting one day, a nobleman finds a drunkard, Christopher Sly, asleep outside a tavern in Warwickshire. He decides to play a trick on him, takes him into his house and has Sly dressed and treated as a lord. Sly is presented with a 'wife'. A group of actors arrive and the nobleman asks them to perform for the disguised tinker. The entertainment presented is a **comedy** about a rich Italian gentleman, Baptista Minola and his daughters, Katherina and Bianca. Bianca, the younger daughter, has two suitors, Hortensio and Gremio, but Baptista refuses to allow her to marry until a husband has been found for her elder sister, Katherina, who is considered a bad-tempered shrew. Hortensio and Gremio agree that they will help to find a husband for Katherina and engage the services of tutors for Bianca to curry favour with her father. Meanwhile Lucentio, a well-born young man, arrives in Padua with his servant Tranio. He intends to pursue his education but falls in love with Bianca, disguising himself so that he can be engaged as her tutor, while Tranio takes on his identity. Petruchio, a friend of Hortensio, also arrives in Padua at this time. He is seeking a wealthy wife and agrees to court and marry Katherina. Hortensio assumes the disguise of a music teacher and is presented to Baptista in this role by Petruchio.

The courtship of Katherina is brief and rough, and Petruchio behaves very eccentrically at his wedding; the bride is carried off to her new home immediately after the ceremony. Here Petruchio sets about taming his wife. She is starved, kept awake and refused new clothes; essentially Katherina is tormented and deprived until she submits to her husband's will and acknowledges his right to rule her. Meanwhile, Baptista has promised Bianca to Tranio (whom he believes to be Lucentio). Tranio has persuaded a pedant to pretend to be his father so that a large dowry can be guaranteed; the aim is to outbid Gremio, who is still pursuing Bianca's hand in marriage. However, Lucentio's real father, Vincentio, arrives in Padua, and the real Lucentio has married Bianca secretly. Baptista and Vincentio are not amused, but are finally persuaded to accept their children's actions. Petruchio and Katherina have returned to Padua and at a wedding feast the success of the wife-taming is revealed publicly: Katherina demonstrates that she is a more obedient and dutiful wife than either her sister or the wealthy widow whom Hortensio has married, neither of whom come when their husbands call for them.

INDUCTION

SCENE 1 Sly is thrown out of the inn. A nobleman decides to play an elaborate trick on him

A tinker, Christopher Sly, is ejected from an alehouse by its Hostess and falls asleep in a drunken stupor on the ground, where he is found by a nobleman who has just returned from hunting. To amuse himself the Lord decides to play a trick on Sly, who will be carried off to his house, dressed magnificently and served delicious food. The intention is to see whether a 'monstrous beast' (line 32) can be persuaded to accept such a wild transformation in his circumstances as reality rather than a dream. The Lord adds further details to his plan; his huntsman is given elaborate instructions about the presentation of Sly's room and when he wakes up the tinker is to be told that he is a 'mighty lord' (line 63) who has been 'lunatic' (line 61) for fifteen years, to the chagrin of his wife and the rest of his household. When a troupe of strolling players arrive they are incorporated into the scheme. The actors are asked to perform for Sly (whom they are told is an eccentric lord, given to odd behaviour). The Lord then sends a servant to his page, Bartholomew, who is to act out the role of Sly's wife. Bartholomew is to pretend to be overjoyed to see 'her' noble husband returned to health and sanity. The Lord intends that his own presence should serve to dampen any excessive merriment caused by what ensues.

This first scene of the **Induction** introduces a number of themes or issues that are mirrored in the taming plot. It is appropriate that the Lord has just returned from hunting; later we will learn that Petruchio, whom some critics see as a fortune-hunting rascal, comes 'to wive it wealthily in Padua; / If wealthily, then happily in Padua' (I.2.74–75). Having secured Kate he sets about taming her, as a Lord might tame a falcon (see Imagery). Bianca's suitors might also be viewed as fortune-hunters, each seeking Baptista Minola's 'treasure' (II.1.32). The Lord's elaborate joke at Sly's expense foreshadows the taming plot too: can Petruchio bring about a radical change in his 'monstrous beast' (line 32), make her 'conformable' (II.1.271)? We are introduced to ideas about role-playing; the Lord and his servants will adopt disguises in order to deceive Sly. Later, we watch as the male characters in both plot and subplot change their clothes and identities to pursue their aims. Layers of illusion become more complicated as the troupe of players arrive; the actors, who earn their living by deception, are themselves deceived by the Lord, who assures them that Sly is a nobleman. Here, the Induction is self-consciously theatrical, a point reinforced by the discussion of the role Bartholomew is to play: here we have a boy actor playing a male servant playing a lady. A **feminist** critic might assert that this self-conscious drawing of attention to the role of the boy actor suggests that women's roles and behaviour are constructed by the (male) playwright. Shakespeare deliberately uses his Induction to indicate that we are watching a topsy-turvy world. We might feel that it is implied that Katherina's shrewishness is part of the illusion; her 'unnatural' behaviour will be beaten out of her so that she becomes a more 'conformable' woman and wife, just as Sly (and his 'wife') will be returned to their natural states when the Lord's whim is played out. It is also noticeable that Petruchio adopts outrageous clothes and eccentric behaviour in his 'taming school' and uses them to impose his will on the Paduans, forcing them to accept his version of events. This is hinted at by Sly, who will be convinced that he is not dreaming when he wakes up. It is noticeable that the nobleman is to retain the upper hand however; even when Sly is licensed to behave like a lord, the Lord will be on hand to 'abate the over-merry spleen / Which otherwise would grow into extremes' (lines 134–35). Do these lines hint at the control Petruchio is to exert? The importance of social rank and identity are clearly highlighted in the Induction, and the role of language and its link to power is suggested too. Sly's rank and identity are to be transformed and he is to be offered power: but only for a limited period and only as a joke. Note how Sly's language becomes transformed when he 'becomes' a lord; from the colloquial 'I'll feeze you, in faith' (line 1) to the more elevated and elegant courtly tone he adopts in the second scene of the Induction. This transformation will be mirrored in Katherina, who begins the play making what is characterised by the male Paduans as an infernal din, only to be silenced, before speaking with what many would argue is her husband's voice, in the final scene. Her famous final capitulation is perhaps an endorsement of male power and supremacy, just as the trick set up in the Induction is a Lord's whim. The relationship between master and servant enacted in this scene hints at the resolution of the taming plot; for all the subversion that is implied by having Sly made lord for a day, we know he has no real power. The servants who wait on him are in fact serving their real lord, just as Petruchio's complaining servant Grumio serves his master, and Tranio acts the role of Lucentio to assist with his master's plans. (See also Textual Analysis, Text 1.)

1 **feeze** (dialect) beat, flog, drive off

4 **Richard Conqueror** in his ignorance, Sly mixes up William the Conqueror and Richard Lion-Heart

5 ***paucas pallabris*** (Spanish) a mispronunciation of a Spanish phrase meaning 'few words'

Sessa be quiet!

7 **denier** small French coin

Go by, Saint Jeronimy a misquotation from a popular revenge tragedy by Thomas Kyd, *The Spanish Tragedy* (1594). The hero of this play is Hieronimo (Jeronimo)

9 **third-borough** constable

14 **tender** look after

15 **emboss'd** foaming at the mouth through exhaustion

16 **brach** bitch

37 **banquet** dessert

38 **brave** dressed in fine clothes

55 **diaper** towel

99 **the veriest antic** a most eccentric person

100 **buttery** room where liquid refreshments were kept and served

SCENE 2 Sly is duped into believing he is a lord and settles down to watch the play that has been provided to entertain him

When he wakes up Sly initially refuses to accept that he is a lord and calls for a pot of ale. He is gradually persuaded to accept that he is a nobleman when he is told of his wealth, possessions and beautiful wife. He is asked whether he wishes to hear some music, or would he prefer to go hunting or hawking? Bartholomew the page enters in disguise and announces that he is Sly's 'wife in all obedience' (line 108). Sly immediately suggests they go to bed, but his 'wife' informs him that doctors have decreed that this would 'incur your former malady' (line 123). A messenger says the same doctors have suggested that an entertainment would be a suitable way to drive away the melancholy that Sly's illness might have caused. Sly agrees to watch the play and calls on his 'wife' to sit by his side.

The action continues with the deception outlined in the previous scene. When Bartholomew declares that he is the drunkard's obedient wife we are offered a glimpse of what Katherina will become. Or are we? Is Shakespeare suggesting that the obedient wife is a fiction, just as Bartholomew the wife and Sly the Lord are impostors? We are reminded that we are watching an illusion when the actors take their places on the stage to entertain Sly.

The critic Stevie Davies makes some interesting comments about the classical references made in this scene, when Sly's 'possessions' are described to him, particularly the artworks. She notes that the pictures all depict scenes of transformation and sexual violence, and links these pictures to the relationship between hunting and 'the sexual chase' (see Critical History, on Current Approaches). These ideas can clearly be linked to what is to happen in the play the troupe are to perform. It is noticeable that Sly is prevented from taking his 'wife' to bed: Petruchio will refuse to consummate his marriage until Katherina has conformed and capitulated.

1 **small ale** cheapest weak beer
2 **sack** white Spanish wine
3 **conserves** candies or sweetened fruit
19 **cardmaker** a person who made combs for spinning wool
20 **bear-herd** the person who had charge of the performing bear
21, 22 **Hacket, Wincot** place names in Warwickshire
23 **sheer ale** strong beer
36 **Apollo** the Greek god of music
40 **Semiramis** An Assyrian goddess, a legendary oriental beauty
42 **trapp'd** decorated with ornaments

46 **welkin** a poetical term for the sky

51–61 **Adonis painted ... tears are drawn** the tales behind the artworks described in this scene can be found in Ovid's poetry. Adonis was a young huntsman, who was loved by Venus. He preferred hunting to love

55 **Io** a priestess loved by Jupiter, whom he changed into a heifer

58 **Daphne** a nymph pursued by Apollo, who was turned into a laurel by the gods

88 **present her at the leet** charge her at the assizes (manorial court)

89 **stone jugs and no seal'd quarts** sealed quarts were stamped with an official seal; stone jugs were different sizes and held different amounts

106 **goodman** a peasant term for husband

137 **comonty** a mispronunciation of comedy

138 **gambol** dance

tumbling trick example of bawdy innuendo; Sly is eager to take his 'wife' to bed

ACT I

SCENE 1 Baptista Minola refuses to allow his younger daughter, Bianca, to marry until a husband is found for her elder sister, Katherina. Lucentio falls in love with Bianca and changes clothes with his servant, Tranio

Lucentio, the son of Vincentio, a wealthy gentleman of Pisa, has come to Padua to continue his education. He is accompanied by his resourceful servant Tranio, who advises him not to take his studies too seriously: he should enjoy music and poetry as well as philosophy. While Lucentio is wondering what has happened to his other servant, Biondello, Baptista Minola appears with his two daughters, Katherina and Bianca, and Bianca's two suitors, Gremio and Hortensio. Lucentio and Tranio overhear their conversation. Baptista will not allow Gremio or Hortensio to court Bianca until a husband has been found for her elder sister, Katherina. Katherina has a reputation as a bad-tempered scold, who is 'too rough' (line 55) to attract a husband. Gremio and Hortensio clearly find her alarming, and suggest that she is unmarriageable, but Baptista is firm in his resolve. He announces that he is looking for tutors for Bianca.

When he leaves the stage with his daughters, Gremio and Hortensio agree to put aside their rivalry while they attempt to find a suitor for Katherina.

After they have left, Lucentio declares that he has fallen in love with Bianca. Tranio reminds him that a husband must first be found for her 'curst and shrewd' sister (line 180). Master and servant arrive at a solution simultaneously: Lucentio should disguise himself as a schoolmaster so that he can gain admittance to Baptista's house. Meanwhile Tranio will pretend to be Lucentio. They exchange clothes. When Biondello arrives, he is perplexed by the role-reversal that has taken place, but is persuaded to accept that he should now treat Tranio as his master.

A servant asks Sly whether he finds the play entertaining; he replies that it pleases him but he hopes that it will soon be over (he wants to go to bed with his 'wife').

> Katherina may have a reputation as a scold, but she says very little to merit the opprobrium she attracts; in this scene she speaks only twelve lines. Her detractors say far more, suggesting the male characters have the power to define the female, as the Lord had the power to give Sly a new identity in the Induction. However, Kate's few lines give a clear indication that she is not the Elizabethan ideal of the silent woman. Her opening speech and retort to Hortensio suggest that she is impatient and spirited. Is Katherina also contemptuous of men? Certainly, she dislikes her social position: she is the unwanted elder daughter, whose younger sister is desirable. This is degrading and Kate does not like to be publicly humiliated, as her querulous tone indicates. It seems clear that Baptista favours his quiet, apparently obedient child, who pleases him by 'humbly' subscribing to his 'pleasure', making no demands and taking herself off to study her 'books and instruments' (lines 81–2). Note the possessive 'my' Baptista adopts when addressing Bianca; he barely acknowledges Katherina, either speaking as if she were not there, or instructing her to stay outside when he leaves. By way of contrast to her sister, Kate asks questions and demands answers, which she does not get. When she leaves (line 104) it is already plain that her voice is ignored. Her

father prefers to 'commune' with Bianca, suggesting that Kate is not a valued member of the family unit; quite the reverse: she is a troublesome outsider and a thorn in her father's flesh.

Gremio seems to sum up the masculine view of Kate when he says it would be a mercy to find someone who would 'thoroughly woo her, wed her, and bed her, and rid the house of her' (lines 143–5). The phrasing here **ironically** foreshadows Petruchio's brutal, breathless wooing and clearly indicates Kate is a nuisance the men need to be 'rid' of (Tranio's words at line 181 reinforce this idea). The language suggests that in Gremio's – and the other men's – eyes, Kate is barely human. The male characters view Katherina as a threat as well as a nuisance. They are scared of her. She is described as 'too rough' (line 55), 'stark mad or wonderful froward' (line 69), given to 'loud alarums' (line 127). More significantly, she is compared to the devil. This link between the shrewish scold and the devil was frequently made in Elizabethan folklore.

In contrast, the language used to describe Bianca suggests that she conforms to the Renaissance ideal of womanhood; she is silent, 'good', 'sweet', 'this young modest girl' (lines 76, 139, 156). The lovestruck Lucentio compares her to classical beauties, and says that, like a courtly lover, he will 'burn … pine … perish' if he does not 'achieve' her (lines 155–6). No wonder her father is interested in *her* education; *this* daughter is indeed a prize, worth improving so that he can barter her successfully on the marriage market.

In spite of Lucentio's musings, marriage is firmly linked to money in this scene, most explicitly when Gremio ponders the likelihood of finding a mate for Katherina: 'Thinkest thou, Hortensio, though her father be very rich, any man is so very a fool to be married to hell?' (lines 123–5). These lines hint at events to come and set up a sense of anticipation. Having seen Katherina for ourselves, and heard her described as 'hell', we wonder what sort of specimen the man who takes her on will be. It is also abundantly clear that marriage is a financial game played by *men*, who jostle for position; at the moment the father holds all the cards because he has something Bianca's suitors want and a bargain must be struck before they will have a chance to court the 'treasure' (II.1.32). Baptista is wily; Gremio and Hortensio have not only agreed to try to find a husband for Katherina (saving her father the trouble); they will also be footing the bill for Bianca's education. We might see this as a fair financial exchange. It is recognised that Baptista is going to have to provide a large dowry to rid himself of Katherina, so it seems fair that the suitors should contribute to the adornment and improvement of the prize they seek. Lucentio's lovestruck musings are undermined by Tranio's pragmatism: 'I pray, awake, sir. If you love the maid, / Bend thoughts and wits to achieve her' (lines 178–9). Like Hortensio and Gremio, Tranio recognises that one has to *work* for a prize. It might be argued that this is exactly why Petruchio succeeds in his taming school: he outwits Katherina (and the Paduans). At the end of the scene plot and subplot are interwoven and deception is the order of the day as Tranio and Lucentio exchange clothes. Key dramatic ideas – the importance of role-reversal and transformation, and the deceptiveness of appearances – are established here. All the male characters are focused on Bianca, but, ironically they must consider the fate of her irksome sister first. This early comedy has started with unromantic subterfuge and bargaining, as it will proceed.

2 **Padua** an Italian university town; the university was established there in 1228

23 **plash** a puddle or pool

25 ***mi perdonato*** (Italian) pardon me

31 **stoics** those who dislike and shun pleasure, taken from the Greek philosophers, the Stoics, who preached the endurance of suffering

33 **Ovid** the Roman poet of amorous poems used during the wooing of Bianca

34 **Balk** use in conversation

34–8 **logic ... stomach serves you** Tranio outlines the typical academic curriculum studied by the gentleman of the time: rhetoric (the art of argument), mathematics, poetry and metaphysics

38 **stomach** desire or inclination

41 **Gramercies** thanks

pantaloon a stock character from commedia dell'arte; a silly old man

50 **bestow** find a husband for

56 **cart her** prostitutes were carried through the streets on a cart

58 **stale** prostitute or laughing stock

64 **comb your noddle** hit your head

69 **froward** perverse (note how frequently you come across this word in the play); the implication is that froward women are unnatural

78 **peat** pet or favourite child (a term of contempt)

84 **Minerva** the Roman goddess of wisdom; an **ironic** allusion. Bianca is wise, but not in the way Lucentio expects her to be; she knows the value of silence

87 **mew her up** a hawking term meaning to cage

97 **Prefer** recommend

cunning clever

108 **Our cake's dough on both sides** (proverbial) we will both fail

115 **parle** negotiate a truce

127 **alarums** trumpets, signalling the start of battle; the war **imagery** helps us understand how nervous Kate makes the men; ironically, her final speech of submission also includes imagery of war

154 **Anna** the sister and confidante of Dido, Queen of Carthage. She killed herself after suffering unrequited love for Aeneas. The story can be found in Virgil's *Aeneid*

162 ***Redime te captum quam queas minimo*** (Latin) 'get yourself out of captivity as cheaply as possible', from the Roman comedy, *The Eunuch*, by Plautus

168 **the daughter of Agenor** Europa was the daughter of the King of Phoenicia. Jove, disguised as a bull, fell in love with her and carried her off to Crete. From Ovid

180 **shrewd** hard to rule or control; another word that is repeated many times

198 ***Basta*** (Italian) enough

207 **Uncase thee** take off your cloak

248 ***The Presenters above*** those introducing the play were standing above the stage

249 **Saint Anne** the mother of Saint Mary

Scene 2 Petruchio arrives in Padua and agrees to court Katherina

A second visitor, Petruchio, arrives in Padua with his servant Grumio. He has come to visit Hortensio, and is looking for a wealthy woman to marry. Hortensio tells him about Katherina, warning his friend that she is 'shrewd' and 'ill-favoured' (line 59). Petruchio refuses to be put off by her reputation as 'an irksome brawling scold' (line 186) and wishes to be introduced to Katherina's father without delay. Hortensio explains that he is in love with Bianca. Like Lucentio, he decides to adopt a disguise in order to gain admittance to his beloved's house and asks Petruchio to present him to Baptista as a music tutor.

Gremio arrives with the disguised Lucentio, whom he has engaged as a schoolmaster. He expects the young man – 'Cambio' – to plead his cause with Bianca. Hortensio lies to his rival, telling him that he too has found a tutor for 'our mistress' (line 167). Gremio is astonished when he hears that Petruchio is prepared to court and marry the 'wildcat' Katherina (line 194) but agrees to 'bear his charge of wooing' (line 214) with Hortensio. At this point the disguised Tranio appears, announcing that he is another suitor for Bianca's hand. He too says he will 'gratify' (line 271) Petruchio, who, it seems, is to be handsomely rewarded for wooing the scold.

Themes and ideas established in the previous scene are further developed here. The introduction of Petruchio and the discussion of financial arrangements that accompany the talk of wooing Katherina extend our understanding of the marriage market. Another disguise is planned, and Lucentio and Tranio continue with their deception. The opening altercation between Grumio and Petruchio hints at the latter's potential for violence. This quick-fire exchange also foreshadows the wooing of Katherina. We are immediately aware that Petruchio is interested in money; he has 'come abroad' (line 57) to seek his fortune and is breezily unconcerned about the character of his wife-to-be: so long as she is rich he will be satisfied. All his speeches in this scene are confident and direct and many include references to wealth. His brazen self-assurance is summed up by two lines, 'I know she is an irksome brawling scold. / If that be all, masters, I hear no harm' (lines 186–7). Petruchio appears to be a man of action; he restlessly says that he 'will not sleep' (line 102) until he sees Katherina, suggesting he wants to get on with the business of wooing the wildcat as swiftly as possible. Later he adds to the impression of masculine valour he is constructing when he outlines his previous life experiences in a wonderfully energetic speech (lines 197–209). It is clear that, unlike the Paduans, Petruchio is not scared of a woman's tongue. Grumio further enlightens us about his master's character, assuring Hortensio that 'scolding would do little good upon him' because, 'he begin once, he'll rail in his rope-tricks' (lines 108–11). These lines are a clear indication that Petruchio will be more of a shrew than Katherina: she has met her match; a man as determined as she is, who has a reputation for powerful talking. And as in the previous scene, there is little romance (none at all in Petruchio's lines). When he speaks disparagingly of Katherina's shrewish tongue he belittles the female voice: later we will watch as Petruchio makes women's words meaningless. By the end of the scene the 'hero' is already speaking of Katherina as part of his goods and chattels, as he will on the wedding day. He warns Tranio off with these words, 'Sir, sir, the first's for me, let her go by' (line 254). Petruchio has made his decision and with the force of will he displays in his first scene, he will carry all before him.

7 **rebused** like Sly, Grumio mispronounces words. He means abused

17 **solfa** the notes on the scale

24 ***Con tutto ... trovato*** (Italian) with all my heart

25–6 ***Alla nostra ... Petruchio*** welcome to our house, most honoured Petruchio

27 **compound** settle

28 **in Latin** Grumio's Englishness is comic here; he can't tell Latin from Italian

two and thirty, a pip out the winning score in a card game like cribbage; here it means he is beyond himself

68 **foul** ugly

Florentius' love Florentius appears in John Gower's *Confessio Amantis*. He was forced to marry a hag, but she was transformed into a beautiful woman; Chaucer uses this story in *The Wife of Bath's Tale*. This reference hints at the outcome of the play

69 **Sibyl** Greek prophetess

70 **Xanthippe** the wife of the Greek philosopher Socrates, a renowned scold

72–3 **as rough ... seas** there are a number of sea **images** in Petruchio's speeches; appropriate since he is to behave rather like a pirate ('board her' later on in the same scene is a naval term for an attack on a sea vessel)

77 **aglet-baby** doll

77 **trot** hag

104 **give you over** leave your company

111 **rope-tricks** meaning unclear: possibly rhetoric, the subject Lucentio has supposedly come to learn in Padua. Petruchio proves to be more interested in practice than theory

113–14 **no more eyes ... a cat** a clever **pun** on Kate's name; it might also refer to the cat o' nine tails, a whip used to tame shrewish wives

142 **A proper ... amorous** an **ironic** comment from Grumio; like his master he is describing things as the opposite of what they are

159 **woodcock** a bird that was easy to catch, therefore a byword for stupidity

202 **ordnance** artillery

208 **a chestnut in a farmer's fire** chestnuts explode when roasted. Young lovers used chestnuts to find out how their love would turn out; if the nuts exploded in the fire it meant that there was quarrelling ahead

209 **bugs** bogeys or bugbears, hobgoblins used to frighten children

242 **Leda's daughter** Helen of Troy, who married Menelaus, King of Sparta. When she ran away with Paris, son of the King of Troy, she caused the Trojan Wars

247 **jade** an inferior, worn-out horse

255–6 **labour ... Alcides' twelve** a reference to the twelve labours of Hercules (Alcides), who had extraordinary strength

271 **gratify** pay or reward

275 **quaff carouses** drink toasts

280 ***ben venuto*** (Italian) host, literally, 'welcome'

ACT II

SCENE 1 Petruchio 'woos' and 'wins' Katherina

The scene moves to Baptista's house, where Katherina is tormenting her sister. She has tied Bianca's hands and taunts her, demanding to know which of her suitors she likes best. Baptista releases his younger daughter and tells her to go inside. Katherina storms off, vowing revenge, and angry with her father because he appears to favour Bianca; she is also concerned about being humiliated if her younger sister is allowed to marry first. Bianca's suitors arrive, accompanied by Petruchio, who immediately requests permission to court his 'fair and virtuous' daughter Katherina (lines 42–3). The tutors are introduced; Hortensio is 'Litio',

Lucentio, 'Cambio'. Baptista sends them in to his daughters and continues his discussion with Petruchio, who makes enquiries about Katherina's dowry and assures his potential father-in-law that his future wife will be well provided for should he die. Baptista reminds Petruchio that he must win his daughter's love, and advises him that he should be 'armed for some unhappy words' (line 139) when he meets Kate. Petruchio refuses to be perturbed by yet another warning. With exquisite timing, Hortensio reappears, '*with his head broke*' (after line 137); Katherina has beaten him with his lute. Baptista goes in to fetch his elder daughter and Petruchio declares his intention to 'woo her with some spirit when she comes!' (line 169).

The wooing is indeed rough; the pair of 'lovers' argue in (sexual) puns, with Petruchio insisting firmly that he is the man 'born to tame' Kate (line 269). When Katherina strikes him, Petruchio restrains her physically; a visual **symbol** of his intentions. Baptista enters with Gremio and Tranio. Petruchio announces boldly that he has won Kate, while the latter castigates her father for permitting 'one half lunatic' to court her (line 280). Baptista allows himself to be convinced that Petruchio speaks the truth in spite of his daughter's obvious outrage and agrees that the wedding should take place the following Sunday. He then barters with Bianca's two suitors. Tranio outbids Gremio but is expected to provide a guarantee of the dowry he has offered. Alone on stage, Tranio – resourceful as ever – sees that he must set about finding 'a father call'd suppos'd Vincentio' to back up the promises he has made (line 401).

The first part of the scene shows Katherina at her worst. Her violent behaviour is meant to be understood as a sign of her shrewish nature. Critics have made much of her abuse of Bianca, with some suggesting that the heroine's interest in her sister's suitors shows a subconscious desire to be married herself. Certainly Kate is concerned that she will be publicly humiliated, shown by her words to her father: 'she must have a husband, / I must dance barefoot on her wedding-day, / And for your love to her lead apes in hell' (lines 32–4). These lines are an allusion to the idea that unmarried women were said to lead apes into hell because they had no children. The opening exchanges in II.1 suggest sibling rivalry, as well as parental favouritism, which was established earlier. Although we will not view Katherina favourably, it is hard not to feel some sympathy for her. Bianca's line, 'So well I know my duty to my elders' (line 7) can seem smug and sanctimonious, and her father's crude description of her, delivered to Kate's face, 'thou hilding of a devilish spirit' (line 26) is unkind. We can understand Kate's desire to 'find occasion of revenge' (line 36). It is **ironic** that Kate draws attention to her sister's silence; it 'flouts' (line 29) Katherina here, but it is Bianca's speech and unexpected disobedience that will vex her husband in the final moments of the play.

Kate's sulky, stormy behaviour and physical abuse of Bianca prepare us for the encounter she is to have with Petruchio later in the scene, as does her abuse of Hortensio. Baptista's weary rhetorical question at line 37 also helps to prepare us for Petruchio's entrance. The new arrival's appearance will prove to be an antidote to his grief. The incongruity between what we have just seen of Katherina and Petruchio's opening remark, 'Pray, have you not a daughter / Call'd Katherina, fair and virtuous?' (lines 42–3) signals Shakespeare's comic intentions for the wooing, as does Baptista's blunt response, 'I have a daughter, sir, call'd Katherina' (line 44). We see the first glimpse of Petruchio's taming methods here. Throughout the wooing and wedding, he will doggedly assert that Kate is mild and meek, the opposite of what she appears to be. There are different ways of interpreting Petruchio's absurd construction of 'Conformable' (line 271) Katherina. Is he presenting the heroine with a model of behaviour that she must follow in order to take her place by his side in society? Is he seeking to liberate or dominate? Or is this simply an example of a highly skilled actor taking on a role? Perhaps we are to begin to see the fortune-hunter as a teacher at this point; he brings the disguised Hortensio to assist in the education of his bride to be. Note the difference between the polite and formal way in which the men all greet one another, and the boisterous and far from polite banter that Petruchio engages in with Katherina.

Whatever disquiet a modern audience might feel about the idea of a man taming and changing a woman, we are certainly supposed to laugh at Petruchio's elaborate, polite descriptions of Katherina's virtues, which are at odds with the businesslike tone the hero adopts after 'Cambio' and 'Litio' have been sent indoors. From this point onwards it is impossible to avoid the conclusion that female education is intended to improve a woman's prospects on the marriage market. In all the talk of dowries and estates, and Petruchio's abrupt declaration that he cannot come to woo every day, there is no hint of romance. Only Baptista's feeble insistence that Petruchio must obtain his daughter's love suggests that marriage is more than a business transaction, and we are unlikely to be convinced by the father's late, brief concern for his daughter's feelings. Quite the contrary: we will recognise that, as Petruchio says, commenting on the likelihood of his engaging Kate's affections, 'that is nothing' (line 130). Significantly, Petruchio then launches into a description of his 'peremptory' (line 131) qualities, drawing attention to the fact that she *will* yield to him. The stage is set for the battle of the sexes, which is even more eagerly anticipated when Hortensio enters '*with his head broke*'.

Is Petruchio looking forward to meeting Katherina? It is possible to interpret his statements at line 160 as conveying genuine eagerness to meet a 'lusty wench'. But it is equally possible to feel that Shakespeare is simply aiming for laughs; perhaps this is yet another droll remark at Katherina's expense, intended to provoke mirth, and not a sign that the hero secretly wants a strong-minded female companion (the rest of the play suggests that this is exactly what Petruchio *doesn't* want). If we wish to see this line as part of Petruchio's character development, then I suggest we should read these words as an indication that the hero eagerly anticipates taming his bride to be; he knows he will enjoy asserting himself in a rough wooing. His **soliloquy** suggests a bright confidence about his prospects, as we are further informed about the methods Petruchio will use to 'woo her with some spirit' (line 169). The final line can be read as a definite indication of a strong will: Petruchio expects his words to prevail and when he speaks Katherina will listen and submit. He knows there will be a tussle, but he will emerge victorious. This soliloquy adds to the anticipation the audience will be feeling about observing the first meeting of the two protagonists. Note the repeated references to speaking in this soliloquy, hinting that Petruchio will 'out talk' Kate: 'say' appears five times, and there are eight other verbs describing speaking.

The wooing scene is undoubtedly intended to be comic, as the playful and witty repetition of Katherina's name suggests, although one critic, J.D. Huston, has described it as 'nothing less than psychological rape'. Petruchio's familiar and repeated use (and some would say abuse) of Katherina's name also confirms his authority: he has the power to define his chosen bride. By referring to her as 'my super-dainty Kate' (line 188) Petruchio demonstrates his right to possess her. The food **imagery** objectifies Katherina as a morsel to be eaten for his enjoyment. Throughout the rest of the scene there are many other lines that demonstrate the male's physical, mental and verbal authority and superiority. Immediately prior to her father's reappearance we see where the toying with Kate's name will lead: she is to be brought 'from a wild Kate to a Kate / Conformable as other household Kates' (lines 270–1). The impersonality of these two lines suits Petruchio's project: he wants a wealthy bride, and is confident that he can make the Kate he has chosen conform with his standards for a wife. The fact that Katherina has come off worse in the exchanges that precede this firm declaration of what will be suggests that the shrew is going to be tamed. Petruchio remains resolute and businesslike: 'setting all this chat aside' he says as he moves on to 'plain terms': 'your father hath consented / That you shall be my wife, your dowry 'greed on; / And will you, nill you, I will marry you' (lines 261–4). The force and assurance of the modal verbs and the 'nill you' demonstrate the bridegroom's determination to have things his way. It is interesting, however, that Shakespeare then adds this line for Petruchio, 'I am a husband for your turn' (line 265). Is there a suggestion that we should see these two as a good match? This is perhaps the only hint that Kate might have some needs. However, the phrase 'Thou must be married to no man but me' (line 268) reinforces the male's power; he marries, she is to be married. Kate is the passive victim.

Her passivity is demonstrated forcefully when her father returns and she is rendered silent, no doubt outraged by the enormous presumption of Petruchio.

Not that Katherina doesn't attempt to assert her own point of view: she speaks with spirit and contempt, as we would expect. She is almost as quick-witted as her combatant and **puns** with the same alacrity that Petruchio demonstrates. But we know that she has lost when she strikes him and he retorts 'I swear I'll cuff you, if you strike again' (line 218). As in her exchange with Bianca, Katherina's physical violence is ultimately a sign of impotence. She may defiantly declare, 'I care not' (line 233), but she is forced to stay and listen when she would rather leave (see line 235). In spite of his conventional praise of her virtues and beauty, Petruchio's behaviour is aggressive and not lover-like (in a courtly sense) or gentlemanly. Indeed, it is possible to read this 'praise' as ridicule. The descriptions of Kate suggest she does not conform to Elizabethan ideals of physical attractiveness; she is not fair-skinned or light haired. Instead, she seems to resemble a country-bumpkin with her brown-tanned skin. Petruchio's initiation of the sexual punning that occurs between lines 200–26 clearly demonstrates the male's sexual and physical superiority, and a very conventional view of women's roles. Women are 'made to bear'. The conclusion of this line, 'and so are you' is a warning: Katherina will be forced to conform (line 200). Altogether, it is impossible to imagine a less romantic wooing than the meeting of Petruchio and Katherina. He threatens, mocks and talks down his 'lover' in bawdy and assertive language, refusing to admit her voice at all. We see that Petruchio has the power to assert his own view of reality, which he can persuade others to accept. In spite of the fact that there is no proof that his daughter looks favourably on her perverse suitor, Baptista agrees to the wooer's terms. Petruchio's reputation as a powerful talker is well deserved.

13 **Minion** spoilt favourite (from French 'mignon')

26 **hilding** baggage, jade

29 **flouts** challenges

38 ***Cambio*** the name, appropriately, means exchange

54 **entrance to my entertainment** this is a theatrical **metaphor**. Petruchio brings in the disguised Hortensio as his 'entrance fee'

73 **Baccare** (corrupt Latin) stand or get back

80 **Rheims** a university was founded here in the sixteenth century

126 **specialities** specific contracts

127 **covenants** promises

147 **break her to the lute** teach her to play the lute; to break an animal (e.g. a wild horse) is to tame it

156 **pillory** a punishment; stocks for the head and wrists

180 **banns** announcement of marriage, read in church

189 **dainties are all Kates** a **pun** on Kate's name: Kate/cake

197 **movable** a piece of furniture

200 **women are made to bear** to bear children; women's roles are sharply defined in this play

204 **swain** a rustic fool

206 **Should ... buzz** another example of word-play; be/bee, buss/buzz – to kiss

buzzard this word has two meanings: an idiot or a bird of prey

208 **turtle** a turtle dove (**symbol** of love); also easy prey for a buzzard

216 **tongue in your tail** Petruchio is being deliberately obscene with this reference to cunnilingus

223 **coxcomb** fool (a coxcomb was associated with the court jester)

225 **craven** a cock that refused to fight (a coward)

227 **crab** crab-apple, sour tasting – sour person

252 **Dian** Diana was the Greek goddess of hunting and chastity

257 **extempore** impromptu or spontaneous

265 **for your turn** to suit you

271 **Conformable** passive and obedient

household Kates still punning on Kate's name: domestic cats. Note the extensive use of animal **imagery** in this scene (see Themes & Imagery)

277 **dumps** low spirits

283 **Father** note Petruchio's confidence; he already speaks to Baptista as if he were married to Katherina

288 **Grissel** patient Griselda, a byword for female obedience (see Chaucer's *A Clerk's Tale*)

289 **Lucrece** Lucrece killed herself after the tyrannical king of Rome, Tarquin raped her; see Shakespeare's *The Rape of Lucrece* (1594)

306 **meacock** timid or effeminate

ACT II: SCENE 1 continued

332 **Skipper** a half-wit or a youngster

340 **plate** silver

341 **lave** wash

342 **Tyrian** costly purple cloth; the dye was made at Tyre

344 **arras counterpoints** counterpanes or bedspreads from Arras in northern France

346 **boss'd** decorated

350 **milch-kine** dairy cows

362 **ducats** common currency in Europe, first issued by the Duke of Apulia

363 **jointure** settlement

367 **argosy** merchant ship

371–2 **galliases ... galleys** types of ships

378 **outvied** appropriately this is a gambling term, meaning out-bid

383 **cavil** unimportant quibble or objection

398 **fac'd it with a card of ten** another gambling **metaphor**, from card-playing; the implication is that one of the players is bluffing

400 **suppos'd Lucentio** a direct reference to the source play *I Suppositi* (see Structure)

ACT III

SCENE 1 'Cambio' and 'Litio' woo Bianca

Meanwhile, the disguised suitors have been attempting to woo Bianca, who refuses to be treated like a schoolchild by the two rivals; she decides which of her tutors should be allowed to give the first lesson. 'Litio' loses out to 'Cambio'. Ostensibly translating Ovid, Lucentio reveals his true identity and is offered some hope by Bianca, who rejects Hortensio when he offers her instruction in music. When Bianca is called away to help with the preparations for her sister's wedding, Hortensio declares that he is suspicious of 'Cambio' and adds that he will look elsewhere for a wife if his beloved is prepared to cast her 'wandering eyes on every stale' (line 88).

The wooing of Bianca is in sharp contrast to the wooing of Katherina. Here the men do not really have the upper hand, although they work hard to exert themselves. In spite of the fact that she is idealised by her suitors as a perfect, modest maiden, there are clear signs that Bianca possesses a strong will. Her first two lines suggest that she will make her own decisions: 'Why, gentleman, you do me double wrong / To strive for that which resteth in my choice' (lines 16–17). It can be argued that the command she shows in this scene – deciding whom to listen to and how much she will hear and 'learn' – mirrors the control Petruchio exerted over her sister. It is thus **ironic** that Lucentio and Hortensio should try to woo Bianca with typical courtly methods: music and poetry. We have begun to suspect that the goddess they see is not the real Bianca. This scene presents us with another example of the deceptiveness of appearances and it is ironic that the disguised wooers fail to look beyond Bianca's pleasing exterior. Their romantic approach is undermined by the suitors themselves, who squabble like schoolboys over who should 'teach' 'The patroness of heavenly harmony' (line 5). A more prosaic reality breaks through in other ways. Bianca is shrewdly cautious about Lucentio's intentions, as indicated by line 49, 'In time I may believe, yet I mistrust.' And at the end of the scene Hortensio is decidedly unromantic when he announces peevishly that he will 'be quit with' Bianca if she casts her 'wandering eyes on every stale'. Finally, it is highly ironic – and inappropriate – that the love-lorn Lucentio should attempt to woo Bianca with Ovid's poetry. Critics have pointed out that the work he quotes from can be can read as a rather cynical manual for seduction and is certainly not a romantic tract. It seems that Shakespeare is intent on undermining traditional notions of romance in this play.

4 **pedant** schoolmaster

15 **braves** taunts

18 **breeching scholar** a schoolboy in breeches, who deserves a whipping

28–9 ***Hic ibat ... celsa senis*** (Latin) Here flowed the Simois, here is the Sigeian land, here stood the royal palace of old Priam (the King of Troy), from *Heroides* by Ovid

30 **Construe** translate

36 **beguile** deceive

38 **The treble jars** the topmost string is out of tune

43 **presume not ... despair not** Bianca proves that she is as adept as Lucentio in acting out the role of courtly lover

48 **Pedascule** petty schoolmaster

50–1 **Aeacides ... grandfather** Lucentio returns to Ovid. Aeacides is also called Ajax

58 **in three parts** for three voices

69 **past my gamut** beyond elementary teaching; in the Tudor period the gamut (order of notes in the scale) was six

75 **clef** musical key

76 **show pity or I die** more fitting courtly sentiments; earlier Lucentio said he would perish and die if Bianca did not love him; note how different Lucentio's approach is from Petruchio's: here there is a suggestion that the female has some power to choose

88 **stale** a decoy-pigeon used in hawking

89 **list** want or wish

ranging straying; note that the **metaphors** Hortensio employs here are similar to the hawking terms associated with Petruchio, hinting that he will settle for the wealthy widow

SCENE 2 Katherina and Petruchio are married. Petruchio departs with his bride immediately after the ceremony

Baptista, Katherina and the wedding guests await the arrival of the tardy bridegroom. Katherina is anxious and angry that she has been made a fool of by a man who 'never means to wed where he hath woo'd' (line 17). When Tranio attempts to comfort her, she leaves weeping, followed by Bianca. As Baptista is sympathising with his daughter, Biondello rushes in with the news that Petruchio is approaching, in fantastic garb, riding an old horse and attended by a servant, whose appearance is as inappropriate as his master's. Upon his arrival Petruchio behaves eccentrically. Refusing to change his clothes, he is impatient to greet, marry and kiss his bride as swiftly as possible. Baptista and the guests follow him off stage. Tranio and Lucentio discuss the latter's progress with Bianca and the possibility of an elopement. Before long, Gremio reappears and describes the marriage ceremony. We learn that Petruchio behaved outrageously in church; swearing at and cuffing the priest, throwing wine at the sexton and kissing Katherina violently 'with such a clamorous smack / That at the parting all the church did echo' (lines 177–8). When the wedding party returns Petruchio announces that he must leave with his bride immediately, ignoring all pleas that he should stay for the wedding feast. Kate attempts to defy her husband and is determined to remain behind, but she is overruled. Declaring she is his property, Petruchio warns the party against trying to obstruct him as he 'defends' his wife and makes his leave. The remaining guests are bemused and puzzled; Bianca observes that 'being mad herself' Katherina has been 'madly mated' (line 242). Bianca and 'Lucentio' (Tranio, disguised) are to take Kate and Petruchio's places at the feast.

This scene is a comic *tour de force*, with many moments of high **farce**. Shakespeare sets up the visual comedy (Petruchio's appearance and dramatic exit with his bride) with elaborate descriptions from Biondello and Gremio, which make us eager to observe the interaction between the incongruous couple. The opening exchanges serve the same purpose: will Petruchio arrive? How will he behave? What will he say? After the rough wooing, we do not expect the wedding to pass off without incident. We are not disappointed.

Katherina's anxiety has been interpreted as a sign of her desire to conform: now that she has been presented with a man who will take her on, she sincerely wishes to be married. She certainly continues to dread social disgrace. **Ironically**, what is most striking about this scene is the way in which Petruchio refuses to conform to society's expectations of a bridegroom (just as, to the onlookers, Kate is an unconventional bride). The hero's tardiness suggests subversion immediately. He continues to ignore social conventions completely, as he did when he wooed Kate. Petruchio's dress, method of transport, behaviour in the church and refusal to stay for the feast are all subversive (and often hilarious on stage). Critics have suggested that Petruchio is attempting to demonstrate to Katherina that, really, *she* is at fault.

It is clear that Petruchio is playing a role throughout this scene: he is the 'mad-brain rudesby' (line 10), more bizarre and outlandish than his wife. His transformation into 'frantic fool' (line 12) demonstrates that Katherina too will be transformed and find another role to play. Petruchio's words and actions foreshadow his taming methods when he is at home in Act IV. We are intended to see that the bridegroom is deliberately killing his wife in her own humour.

However, as in I.1, Katherina's shrewishness amounts to little more than voicing her feelings and we are likely to sympathise with her situation. She is forced to wait passively for her 'merry man' (line 14) to arrive and claim her, and then has to resort to pleading with him after the ceremony. It is only when he ignores her, addressing his servant as he makes preparations to leave ('Grumio, my horse', line 202) that Katherina tries to exert her own will to 'please myself' (line 210). By now we know her indignation is pointless: Petruchio has been allowed to marry her on his own terms, and will undoubtedly do as he pleases. Kate has been humbled in this scene, and will be further shamed until she becomes the wife her husband wants. Here we are presented again with the idea that the male is superior and possesses all the power. Petruchio's speech at line 220 makes this abundantly clear; Katherina is now told in no uncertain terms who her master is (lines 226–31).

These lines reiterate the idea that the male can define the female, as Kate is told how she should behave as a piece of Petruchio's property. She has been passed from one owner (her father) to another (her husband), and must accept that her old ways, which caused Baptista so much grief, are no longer acceptable. We will recall these lines when Katherina offers her public speech of submission at the end of the play.

The audience at the wedding have colluded with Petruchio. In spite of Baptista's disquiet when he sees Petruchio's garb ('But thus, I trust, you will not marry her', line 113) and Gremio's amazement at what occurs in the church ('Such a mad marriage never was before', line 180), Petruchio gets what he wants, says what he wants, leaves when he wants and continues to assert his own version of reality, which includes furthering the illusion that he has 'a most patient, sweet, and virtuous wife' (line 193). The final absurd fiction he creates, when he 'rescues' Katherina from thieves, seals the supreme command of events he has shown throughout III.2.

As in previous scenes, the other characters are forced to react to and accommodate the dominant male. They comment on Petruchio's behaviour and appearance, but do not really challenge him. They – and we, the audience – are forced to marvel at the protagonist's swaggering, boisterous display. As well as creating an obedient wife, Petruchio has also reconfirmed his masculine valour, amusingly setting himself up as a knight defending his lady-love. His exaggerated posturing further undermines the ideals of courtly love that Lucentio espoused in I.1. As the newly weds leave the stage, we are not likely to agree with Gremio's assertion that 'Petruchio is Kated' (line 243). On the contrary, we understand that the bridegroom's taming methods will be highly effective. At the end of the scene Baptista attempts to reassert the social conventions that have been overturned so dramatically when he replaces the bride and groom at the feast with 'stand ins'. Perhaps these final lines are a sign that Kate is on the road to conformity. (See also Textual Analysis, Text 2.)

10 **rudesby** rude, rough fellow

42 **thrice turned** turned inside out three times (to conceal the wear)

45 **chapeless** without the metal plate on the scabbard to cover the point of the sword

46 **points** laces

hipped with broken hips

47 **of no kindred** not from the same matching pair

48–53 **glanders ... shoulder shotten** this horse has an impressive collection of ailments: swollen legs, jaundice, strained shoulders, tumours, loss of balance, worms

54 **near-legged before** knock-kneed

58 **crupper** the rear part of the saddle, used by passengers

68 **footboy** page

93 **wondrous monument** a bad omen

97 **unprovided** badly or inappropriately dressed

98 **doff this habit** take off these garments

138 **steal our marriage** elope

Act iii Scene 2 continued

158 **by gogs-wouns** by God's wounds (Petruchio is cursing inappropriately here)

171 **sops** dregs

209 **you may be jogging ... green** go as soon as you want to (a reference to boots being clean and ready for the journey)

211 **jolly** arrogant (or Kate could be offering an **ironic** comment about her husband)

222 **domineer** riot, lord it

226 **look not big** don't be proud

230 **my ox, my ass, my anything** Petruchio is parodying the ten commandments here

237 **buckler thee** protect you with my sword

243 **Kated** a **pun** on mated/mad – the implication is that bride and groom both share the same bad temper

246 **junkets** delicacies

ACT IV

SCENE 1 Arriving home, Petruchio sets about taming Katherina

Complaining and cold, Grumio arrives home ahead of his master with orders for the other servants; they must light the fire and prepare the house and supper for the arrival of the bride and groom. We learn that the journey has been full of mishaps. When he enters, an enraged Petruchio shouts at the servants for failing to carry out his orders. This overbearing behaviour continues when the meal is served, with Petruchio striking the servants and throwing the 'overcooked' meat at them. Kate – who has wearily attempted to defend the men and calm her husband – is not allowed to eat. Instead she is hurried off to the bedchamber by her perverse bridegroom. When Grumio enquires where his master is, Curtis tells him that Petruchio has been 'Making a sermon of continency' to his dazed wife (line 170). Alone on stage, Petruchio outlines his plan to tame Katherina. He will deprive her of food and sleep and insist that 'all is done in reverend care of her' until she submits to his will (line 191).

As in the previous scene, we are prepared for Petruchio's entrance with informative and descriptive speeches. Grumio's physical abuse of Curtis foreshadows Petruchio's treatment of the servants. His loquacity mirrors his master's verbal dexterity. Grumio's words and actions also hint at his collusion with Petruchio (he will help starve Katherina into submission). His speech at line 64 alerts us to the fact that Kate is losing ground all the time. Not only is Petruchio (as we suspected) 'more shrew than she' (line 76), but Katherina has also suffered the indignity of falling off her horse 'in a miry place', becoming 'bemoiled' (line 67), while her husband 'left her with the horse upon her' (lines 67–8). Is this a mire of her own making? Some critics have argued that we are supposed to view Kate's ill-fortune on the journey as a sign that she will continue to find life difficult and unpleasant until she recognises the folly of her ways. Others argue that the treatment she receives at Petruchio's hands is out of all proportion to her supposed crimes as a scold.

When she does appear, it seems that Katherina's spirit has already been broken. She says very little, and when she speaks she pleads (see lines 143 and 155), making no personal demands. It is perhaps significant that she addresses her husband with the more formal 'you', rather than 'thou', which was a term of intimacy. Has she been cowed? Conversely, Petruchio continues to dominate the other characters on stage physically and verbally, and is a demanding, discontented master. We discover why he is behaving like a domestic tyrant when he is alone on stage at the end of the scene. He has 'politicly begun my reign' (line 175) and intends to maintain his supremacy in order to 'curb' Katherina's 'mad and headstrong humour' (line 196). The **imagery** of falconry he employs reflects his resolute taming methods. It also suggests that Katherina must become obedient so that she is an asset to her master, as a tame hawk reflects its owner's prowess. Some critics have suggested that the careful plan Petruchio outlines will make him suffer as much as his wife: he too must go without sleep in order to 'kill a wife with kindness' (line 195). However, the determined tone of the speech and the impersonality of the hawking **metaphors** and other references to Katherina (who is not once named in this **soliloquy**), would seem to indicate that Petruchio views the educational process he is engaged in, in a detached way. There is no mention of emotion. The protagonist could be speaking of any woman he had chosen to wed who 'will not be obedient' (line 183). The main topic of the speech is masculine control and the necessary methods for achieving it. The last two lines of the scene can be interpreted in different ways. Either Petruchio is asking for assistance (which he does not need: we know his methods are working) or he is boasting (his request is rhetorical). Either way, he is undeniably in charge in his own home.

3 **rayed** dirtied or muddied

5 **a little pot and soon hot** a small man who is easily enraged

37 **cony-catching** deceiving simple people; there is a **pun** on 'catch'

44 **Jacks ... Jills** male and female servants

45 **carpets** coverings for tables and chairs

59 ***Imprimis*** (Latin) first

106 **Cock's passion** an oath, By God's passion

120 **all unpink'd** without proper decoration (ornamental holes pricked in the leather)

121 **link** black material, from torches, used to dye hats

144 **beetle-headed** thick-headed (a beetle was a mallet)

145 **you have a stomach** you are (a) hungry or (b) proud/hot tempered

159 **choler** angry

180 **haggard** wild hawk

183 **bate and beat** flutter and flap the wings

190 **hurly** chaos, disorder

195 **to kill a wife with kindness** (proverbial) this meant that the husband was too indulgent towards his wife, making her disobedient. Petruchio means the opposite of what he says here. There is a popular domestic tragedy by Thomas Heywood, *A Woman Killed with Kindness* (1603)

SCENE 2 Hortensio rejects Bianca. Tranio persuades an old man, the Pedant, to play the role of Vincentio

Hortensio and 'Lucentio' (Tranio) are spying on Bianca and 'Cambio' (Lucentio), who continues to woo his 'pupil'. Tranio professes outrage at the inconstancy of women (line 14). Hortensio reveals his identity and agrees that he too will forswear Bianca; he intends to marry a wealthy widow in three days' time. When he leaves, Tranio tells Bianca and his master what has happened. As they rejoice, Biondello appears with the news that he has found an old man who might be suitable to play the role of the supposed Vincentio. The Pedant is duped by Tranio, who persuades him that he is in danger in Padua. Fearful that he might be executed, the old man gratefully agrees to impersonate Vincentio and 'pass assurance of a dower in marriage' (line 118).

One disguise is cast off and another assumed as deceptions continue to proliferate in the subplot. Essentially, this scene furthers the action. It is clear that Bianca is in control of her own fate and her lover, as we see when Tranio says to Hortensio, 'See how beastly she doth court him' (line 34). This idea is reinforced by her remark about the prospect of Hortensio taming his widow at line 53. Hortensio remains deluded; he believes that he will now be satisfied by 'Kindness in women' (line 41) rather than beauty. His intention to be married to a wealthy widow suggests that he is as much a fortune-hunter as his friend Petruchio. Tranio dominates the final section of the scene, showing that he is as adept as Petruchio at controlling characters and events. We know that Lucentio would be lost without his guidance and cunning. The references to woman-taming and Petruchio in this scene reinforce the protagonist's dominance. It seems that his fame is spreading far and wide as others marvel at his success in transforming Katherina. Plot and subplot become more closely linked as two more couples move closer to matrimony. We will undoubtedly draw comparisons between these pairings.

3 **bears me fair in hand** encourages me

11 **proceeders** a proceeder was a scholar who had moved from a BA to an MA; therefore a quick learner

14 **despiteful** spiteful

20 **cullion** servant/wretch

24 **lightness** fickleness or disloyalty; there is also a **pun** on Bianca's name, which means 'white'

46 **napping** wooing (they are caught in the act of wooing)

57 **tricks eleven and twenty long** another reference to card playing and gambling; this represents a high score. The implication is that there are lots of tricks going on

61 **An ancient angel** an old man

63 **mercatante** (Italian) merchant

83 **stay'd** kept in custody, under arrest. This is the second time this excuse has been used in the subplot; Lucentio told Biondello that he had been forced to change clothes with Tranio to save his life after killing a man

118 **pass assurance** give a guarantee

scene 3 Petruchio continues the taming, rejecting a hat and gown that have been ordered for Katherina

Weary and starving, Katherina begs Grumio to bring her some food. He taunts and teases her with offers of wonderful delicacies, but does not give her anything to eat. Petruchio appears with Hortensio, bearing a dish of meat. When the trio sit down Petruchio tells his friend to eat all the food in an **aside**. Before Kate has had a chance to assuage her hunger pangs, a tailor and haberdasher arrive. Petruchio rejects the hat and gown they have brought, ignoring Katherina's protests: she likes the garments and wishes to keep them. Petruchio abuses the tailor, who boldly defends the gown, saying that he followed the instructions delivered by Grumio. Grumio joins the fray, quibbling with the tailor and defending his own actions. The tailor is dismissed. In an aside Petruchio tells Hortensio to pay him later and sets about lecturing his wife: clothes and outward appearances are not important. Petruchio then announces that they will visit her father, leaving immediately. He deliberately mistakes the time and Kate tries to correct her husband. Petruchio warns her against contradicting him. The trip is cancelled.

There are further examples of **slapstick** and quick-witted verbal comedy in this scene, centring on the interlude with the tailor. Katherina makes a brave attempt to assert herself again, but is completely unsuccessful, because, as Hortensio says, Petruchio 'will command the sun' (line 193) if he chooses. He continues to dominate completely. We can see the efficacy of his taming methods at the beginning of the scene, when Kate outlines what has happened since we last saw her. From her descriptions of life in Petruchio's house it is clear that the plan outlined in IV.1 has been followed to the letter and the young bride's words suggest bewilderment. We are reminded that Kate will be defeated when Grumio denies her food. This is the first of three attempts at breaking her will in this scene: the offer of food is followed by the visit from the tailor and Petruchio's plan to visit her father. On each occasion Kate attempts to assert her own point of view, but her voice continues to be ignored. Grumio has an important role to play in Petruchio's plans for thwarting his wife in this scene and his actions indicate that Kate is isolated. Her impotence grows with each successive scene, despite the fact that she has more to say for herself here.

The scene with the tailor is significant for a number of reasons. Some critics have suggested that Katherina's desire for a gown is further proof that she – secretly or subconsciously – desires to conform to society's codes; she wishes to be attired appropriately as a respectable man's wife. Others suggest that Petruchio withholds the gown because his wife is not yet fit to wear the garb of an obedient wife; she is still, in his word, 'crossing' (line 190) him. The exchange with the tailor adds to our understanding of the theme of appearance and reality.

11 **spites me** angers me

17 **neat's foot** ox or calf's foot

36 **all amort** melancholy or mortified

43 **sorted to no proof** come to nothing

56 **farthingales** hooped skirts

bravery clothing

58 **knavery** nonsense

69 **doth fit the time** is fashionable

82 **custard coffin** crust of a custard pie

87 **masquing stuff** clothing only fit to be worn as a costume at a masque; not proper clothing

91 **censer** incense burner

98 **kennel** street gutter

102 **quaint** skilfully made

103 **puppet** a fool or a dressed up doll

128 **Ergo** (Latin) therefore

132 **loose-bodied gown** this might be an allusion to the kind of dress worn by prostitutes

145 **prove upon thee** a threat to fight in a duel

150 **mete-yard** a yardstick for measuring
167 **habiliments** clothes
177 **furniture** clothing or outfit

Scene 4 Deceived by Tranio and the supposed Vincentio, Baptista agrees to marry Bianca to 'Lucentio'

Tranio ('Lucentio') and the old man, who is dressed to resemble Vincentio, arrive at Baptista's house. Biondello is part of the scheme to deceive Bianca's father; he has told Baptista that 'Vincentio' has recently arrived from Venice. When their prey comes out of his house 'Vincentio' confirms the dowry 'Lucentio' has offered. Baptista does not wish to draw up the wedding agreement in his own home because Gremio is 'hearkening still' (line 53) and agrees to go to 'Lucentio's' lodgings to complete the transaction. The real Lucentio (still disguised as 'Cambio') has been watching his servant Tranio manage the deception so efficiently; as Baptista's servant he is now ordered to inform Bianca 'how she's like to be Lucentio's wife' (line 66). When Tranio leaves with Baptista, Biondello explains what has happened to his rather dim-witted master, and urges him to move along swiftly with his secret marriage to Bianca.

Role-playing through the use of disguises continues to draw our attention to the differences between appearance and reality in the subplot, as the interlude with the tailor in the previous scene highlighted this theme in the taming plot. Like Grumio, Tranio and Biondello assist their master in his matrimonial plans (the former is almost stage-manager in this scene, directing Lucentio's actions). There is **dramatic irony** in the fact that Baptista agrees to marry Bianca to 'Lucentio', commenting that the young people seem to be very much in love, 'Or both dissemble deeply in their affections' (line 42). He unwittingly speaks the truth, having been completely taken in by the wily youngsters. The real Lucentio is as happily deluded as Baptista, believing that he has obtained an obedient and modest wife. His final speech contrasts vividly with the force of Petruchio's speeches before and after his wedding. Note the passivity of this line: 'I may and will, if she be so contented' (line 101). We might also feel that there is a hint of danger in the following line, particularly Lucentio's question: 'She will be pleas'd, then wherefore should I doubt?' The canny audience will be well aware that it is necessary to look beyond appearances, and realise that Lucentio's blissful lack of understanding cannot last much longer. There is further dramatic irony in the fact that the character who seeks to deceive is being deceived himself.

5 **Pegasus** the winged horse, a familiar name for English inns

7 **'longeth to** appropriate to

36 **curious** niggling

49 **affied** engaged

52 **Pitchers have ears** (proverbial) a reference to the possibility that the servants might overhear their plans; **ironic** here, since it is the servants who are plotting

59 **scrivener** a lawyer who drew up legal contracts

70 **One mess** one dish or course

89 ***cum privilegio ad imprimendum solum*** (Latin) this phrase can often be found on the title page of books, it means 'with the right to be sole printer'

103 **roundly go about** approach frankly, or go straight in search of

SCENE 5 Katherina capitulates to her husband. On the road to Padua they meet the real Vincentio

Accompanied by Hortensio and their servants, Petruchio and Kate make their way to Baptista's house in Padua. As contrary as he was in IV.3 Petruchio insists that it is night. When Kate says that it is day he declares that they will all turn round and return home. Katherina finally capitulates and says that she will see the world through her husband's eyes and contradict him no more. Petruchio immediately puts her to the test and greets an old man they meet on the road as if he were a young gentlewoman, urging Kate to do likewise. When she follows his instructions Petruchio scolds her for her 'mad mistaking' (line 48). Katherina apologises for her error. The old man announces that he is Vincentio, on his way to see his son Lucentio in Padua. Petruchio informs him that Lucentio has married Bianca and the travellers continue their journey together. Spurred on by his friend's success, Hortensio is sure that he will be able to tame his widow 'if she be froward' (line 77).

Katherina finally capitulates. But how are we to view her submission? Some would argue that she has been worn down; as Hortensio points out, 'say as he says, or we shall never go' (line 11). Others would argue that her liveliness and wit in this scene suggest that Kate has chosen to take on a new role herself, because she has recognised the 'game' that Petruchio is playing and decided to participate. Certainly it is possible to argue that the encounter with Vincentio is like a game, in which Kate shows off for the amusement of her husband. This meeting also provides Petruchio with an opportunity to test his wife's obedience, and we see that he has won the field completely when he succeeds in getting Katherina to change her mind with the same perverse, lightning speed that he has demonstrated. Some would argue that Kate begins to speak with a new voice in this scene, becoming more eloquent as she greets and then apologises to Vincentio in an exaggerated way, mirroring the style her husband has employed throughout the first four acts of the play. Is this voice Katherina's, or Petruchio's? Has the shrew been silenced, or transformed?

There is an inconsistency in the plot at this point. Petruchio informs Vincentio that his son has married his sister-in-law: he cannot know this, because the secret marriage has not yet occurred. Hortensio's final lines in this scene mirror Lucentio's words at the end of the previous scene: he too remains deluded about his own matrimonial prospects. He says that Petruchio has taught him how to be 'untoward' if his widow is 'froward' (lines 77–8); we know that he does not possess the same steely resolve as his friend and cannot hope to rule anyone. Some would suggest that Hortensio's and Vincentio's presence in this scene, which is public proof of Katherina's obedience, prepares us for her even more public submission in the final scene. It is perhaps appropriate that Katherina's submission is witnessed by other men; she has irked them, and we know that the Paduans feel that Petruchio has carried out a public duty in taking on and taming the shrew. If we are to accept this reading of the scene, then Hortensio's last lines, indeed the whole scene, can be read as proof of the successful outcome of a male wish-fulfilment fantasy. At the same time, we might argue that Shakespeare undermines Petruchio's triumph by closing the scene with his much more feeble friend. And Katherina does not sound humiliated when she speaks in IV.5, even though she follows Petruchio's instructions and seems to make a fool of herself. Is it being suggested that a woman must follow even the most ridiculous commands her husband makes, or are Petruchio's absurd requests **ironic**? The answer depends upon whether we feel Katherina has gained or lost by her submission. Perhaps we cannot view this scene ironically; the reference to the sun and moon was a common analogy used during this period to describe the ideal relationship that should exist between husband and wife. The moon obviously 'follows' the sun and 'mirrors' its behaviour; just as a wife should behave in a way that reflects well on her husband as his subordinate.

7 **what I list** what I please

14 **rush-candle** a flickering candle

23 **the field is won** the battle is won

24–5 **thus the bowl … the bias** this is how things should be; a metaphor from the game of bowls

38–40 **Happy the parents … bedfellow** taken from Ovid

47 **reverend father** a respectable old gentleman or the head of the family

71 **pleasant** joking

75 **jealous** suspicious

77 **Have to** now for

78 **untoward** bad mannered or awkward

ACT V

SCENE 1 'Lucentio' and the supposed Vincentio are unmasked. Baptista and the real Vincentio learn that their children have married in secret. Kate kisses her husband 'in the midst of the street'

Lucentio goes off to marry Bianca, Biondello having informed the couple that the priest is waiting. Petruchio shows Vincentio to his son's lodgings, where they discover the supposed Vincentio, who stoutly refuses to allow them to enter. The Pedant maintains that he is the real

Vincentio. Gremio is standing in the street outside. When Biondello arrives he pretends that he does not know Vincentio, who questions the 'notorious villain' (line 46) angrily. As he beats Biondello the supposed Vincentio calls to Baptista. The real Vincentio is further astonished when Tranio appears, dressed in his son's clothes. He fears Lucentio has been killed by his servant. Tranio calls for Vincentio to be arrested. Gremio tries to intercede; he swears that this new Vincentio is 'the right Vincentio' (line 91) but Baptista has urged the officer to take the 'mad knave' away to prison. When Lucentio and Bianca arrive, Biondello, the supposed Vincentio and Tranio make off as fast as they can: they know they 'are all undone' (line 101). Lucentio begs his father to forgive him and explains to Baptista that he has married Bianca. The deceived fathers are not entirely satisfied, but go into the house together 'to sound the depth of this knavery' (line 126). Petruchio and Katherina have been watching 'this ado' (line 130) and she urges her husband to follow the others. Before they go Petruchio demands a kiss, which Kate reluctantly bestows on him.

The subterfuge of Lucentio and Tranio is uncovered in this scene: the masks come off. The timing of the revelations is significant. Katherina has been transformed, meaning that Petruchio can dispose of his disguise as 'mad-brain rudesby'; in the subplot the characters are forced to dispose of their disguises too. When Tranio and Biondello run away we know that when we next see them they will have returned to their 'proper' roles as servants, just as Kate has now become a 'proper' wife. Events move very swiftly here, but we know that the alarm the real Vincentio feels will not last long. Lucentio is penitent (he kneels to his father, signifying his respect and a return to the correct social order) and his partners in crime make themselves scarce. The threat of subversion is neatly disposed of. Both fathers regain the upper hand at the end of the scene when they go in to the house together. This is as it should be: control has been returned to the right hands. However, we know that Baptista's outwardly obedient daughter has succeeded in duping her father, as Lucentio has deceived his. And it is **ironic** that Lucentio, ever the romantic, claims that 'Love wrought these miracles' (line 113); we know that his success in wooing and wedding Bianca lies with the lady herself, and with Tranio and his clever plotting. The final scene is set up when Gremio retires from the field, content that he should get his 'share of the feast' (line 129). Like Hortensio, he is forced to satisfy himself – realistically – with what he can get. These two suitors' careers as wooers have not been auspicious or in any genuine sense romantic; but as we have already seen in the main plot, romantic ideas about matrimony are no preparation for the reality of wedded life. Interestingly, the scene ends with what some critics view as a moment of genuine affection as Petruchio asks Kate to kiss him. Others see his request as another example of the triumphant husband testing his wife. For those who wish to see this exchange as proof that this match has become a loving marriage, there are two pieces of evidence to point to. The first is that Petruchio and Kate are now in calm waters, observers of the 'ado' caused by Lucentio, his servants and Bianca. They watch the scene unfolding with mutual amusement, and, some might say, a feeling of superiority. The second is the more affectionate terms the married couple use when speaking to one another. Kate is now 'my sweet Kate' (line 137), while he is her 'love' (line 136). Their kiss prepares us for the consummation of the marriage which will be referred to at the end of the play.

out before at the front of the stage, or ahead of the rest

12 **cheer** refreshment, or there might be a suggestion that happy people can be heard ahead

34 **cozen** defraud or cheat

35 **under my countenance** masquerading

40 **crack-hemp** a rascal worthy of being hanged

59 **copatain hat** tall, conical hat

70 **Bergamo** traditionally the home town of servants in Italian comedy

107 **counterfeit supposes** false pretences; another direct reference to the source play (see Structure)

108 **packing** scheming

scene 2 Petruchio wins his wager at the wedding feast. Katherina makes a speech in which she scolds the other women for daring to challenge their husbands' authority

Lucentio welcomes the guests to the banquet, which is being held to celebrate his marriage to Bianca, as well as the marriages of Hortensio and his Widow and Petruchio and Katherina. There is much jesting about shrewish wives and the men engage in a wager. They bet on their wives' obedience. Biondello is sent out to call in the Widow and Bianca. Both refuse to come. Contrary to expectation, Kate obeys Petruchio's summons. She also fetches the other women when required to do so. Baptista is impressed and offers Petruchio a second dowry because his daughter is 'chang'd' (line 115). Petruchio charges Katherina to 'tell these headstrong women / What duty they do owe their lords and husbands' (lines 131–2). Kate lectures the Widow and Bianca, reminding them that they are weak women, who should serve and submit to their menfolk. She offers to place her hand beneath her husband's foot as a token of her duty. Petruchio is delighted with his wife and takes her off to bed.

The final scene begins with Lucentio in complacent mood, and his tone is cheerful and celebratory as he welcomes everyone to the feast. As the characters sit down to 'chat as well as eat' (line 11), it seems that all is resolved and social harmony has been restored, with each person in their rightful place. But we quickly realise that this is not so. Petruchio crows that 'Hortensio fears his widow' (line 16), and a new battle begins. The Widow's challenge to Katherina begins the tussle and introduces the wager: marriage is still linked to money. Now the men bet on the obedience of their wives, reviving the competition that occurred early in the play as suitors fought to be allowed to court Bianca. We are further prepared for the wager by Hortensio and Petruchio urging their wives to put each other down. There are hints that the Widow and Bianca will not be ruled: both assert their own points of view before they leave at line 48. When they have left, the betting begins in earnest. Petruchio employs **images** of hawking, reconfirming the idea that an obedient wife does credit to her master (and in this case, in a financial, as well as a **metaphorical** sense). Shakespeare builds up the dramatic tension which leads to Katherina's long speech of submission with the refusal of the Widow and Bianca to return. Does the audience expect Katherina to refuse to come too? Probably not; in spite of her spirited retorts to the Widow earlier in the scene, we know she has been tamed. The drama of the scene comes from the fact that all the male characters, with the exception of Petruchio, are flabbergasted by Katherina's lecture.

What are we to make of this speech? There are a number of contradictory readings of it. Some critics have argued that it should be delivered in an **ironic** tone; that Katherina is not serious. Others suggest she is playing her husband's game through choice, because it has liberated her (she has found love and a place in society). Others suggest that she does not speak with her own voice here; that a masculine voice has replaced the voice of the scold. Has Shakespeare killed off his original Katherina and replaced her with a female Petruchio impersonator? Certainly the arguments Katherina expounds are 'masculine' and she speaks on cue when requested; she suggests that women should be ruled by men because they are biologically and culturally inferior to the male sex. She also seems to be reconfirming the rights of the patriarchal hierarchy, which decreed that the husband should be the 'head' and 'sovereign' (line 148) of the household, just as the monarch was head and sovereign of the kingdom. Kate's reference to the duty 'the subject owes the prince' (line 156) reinforces this idea. She employs imagery of war too, supporting the idea that Petruchio has won the battle of the sexes. And it is ironic that Kate's longest and most eloquent speech, and the only one that is really heard, is a speech in which she declares her own – and other women's – weaknesses.

But should we believe her? The play does not prove that women are weak, merely that a man has to work hard to subdue a scold. It is ironic that Kate's speech rounding off the play virtually silences the stunned men. Is Shakespeare confirming Petruchio's superiority and triumph, but undermining the other male characters, who remain dupes? Are we to understand that Katherina's speech is a joke against the men? (in spite of Kate's words, and the fact that she seems to be taking on Petruchio's role of tamer when she lectures her 'froward' sisters, the other wives are clearly not malleable).

Those who would argue that Katherina's final speech is not ironic point to the fact that she goes further than saying she is an obedient wife; she offers to place her hand beneath her husband's foot in a gesture that suggests excessive humility. But could we read this as a test of Petruchio? Is she attempting to see how far he will push her? This seems doubtful. As soon as she has finished speaking she gets her reward (a kiss and consummation), just as Petruchio has had his reward for taming her (a second dowry from Baptista). Evidence suggests that Katherina is acting out the role that her husband has cast her in, and that the final lines of the play are not ironic: they all point to the men's admiration for Petruchio's taming methods. Hortensio says unequivocally that he has 'tam'd a curst shrew' (line 189). Or are we to read Lucentio's subsequent line as undermining this? It is indeed 'a wonder' (line 190) that Katherina has delivered this speech: perhaps we are intended to reserve doubts about her future conduct. This is a plausible reading if we consider that one shrew may be vanquished, but another two have revealed their true natures. However hard we try, it is not entirely possible to feel a sense of **closure** at the end of this play. (For further comments on this scene see Textual Analysis, Text 3.)

33 **To her!** go for her!

40 **hasty-witted** quick-witted

46 **bird** prey or game

52 **slipped me** let me off my leash (a hunting metaphor)

56 **at a bay** defending itself against the hounds in the hunt

58 **gird** taunt, a stroke of wit

61 **glance away** rebound

63 **in good sadness** in all seriousness

105 **Swinge** beat

140 **bite the meads** attack the meadows

170 **unable** physically weak

177 **vail your stomachs** throw off your pride and anger

no boot in vain

186 **sped** defeated or finished

187 **hit the white** archaic term and **pun** on Bianca

PART THREE

CRITICAL APPROACHES

CHARACTERISATION

This play contains many elements of **farce**. Great depth cannot be expected from characters who are required by the kind of comedy Shakespeare was writing to move at high speed, without much introspection. The subtlety of characterisation noted in the dramatist's later works is perhaps missing in this early play, and we are not intended to be troubled by the transformations of personality that occur: Kate is required by the genre to change. Having said this, a modern audience is likely to want to analyse the presentation of the characters in detail and seek out and account for any inconsistencies or incongruities that present themselves. It is, of course, legitimate to question Shakespeare's portrayal of his cast in the search for meaning. And it is true that Shakespeare does individualise and transform the stereotypes and stock characters he uses.

PETRUCHIO

For an audience watching and reading the play today, the problem with Petruchio is this: he is outrageous, his behaviour deeply repugnant to modern sensibility, but it is also possible to be enormously entertained by him. The theatrical qualities of the role make him engaging. Petruchio is at times deliberately farcical (the wedding ceremony, his behaviour at his home in Act IV) and he seems to be at the centre of some of the cruder **slapstick** comedy. He is also verbally energetic and linguistically imaginative. His early speeches in I.2 are full of machismo, but they are witty. At times Petruchio is also – perhaps surprisingly – poetic (see his descriptions of Kate's appearance in II.1).The verbal dexterity the protagonist displays can make him, if not endearing, then certainly appealing as a theatrical creation. Our reception of Petruchio depends partly upon the shrewishness of Kate and whether or not he is portrayed as sinister and violent, as well as direct, lively and playful. There are elements of all these qualities in his characterisation.

Petruchio is undoubtedly a fortune-hunter, associated with money and animal taming from the beginning of the play. Within moments of his arrival on stage he has announced that he is seeking a wealthy wife. The action of the play suggests that he is rewarded financially for taming the shrew. His wooing costs are met by the men who wish to get Kate out of the way so that they can court Bianca, and he wins the wager in the final scene. Impressed by the transformation of his daughter, Baptista offers his triumphant son-in-law a second dowry. We might be tempted to feel that Petruchio has been paid for performing a public service, rather than for embarking on a mercantile and risky personal business venture. The protagonist's piratical behaviour continues when he woos Katherina. He sweeps in, overpowers her verbally, threatens to do the same physically, and then sweeps out, nonchalantly announcing when he is prepared to come and claim his bride. We are forced to marvel at the presumption of the man, as eventually, the dumbfounded Katherina does.

As the play progresses Petruchio moves on to new feats of eccentric swaggering, before setting about the taming in earnest in Act IV. The wedding ceremony may look like a game (Gremio's descriptions of the scene in the church and Petruchio's 'mad attire' suggest we should laugh at the incongruity before us), but really, the protagonist is preparing us for his resolute rule, as his speech at the end of III.2 shows (see lines 220–37). The confidence and sense of superiority established in earlier speeches are reconfirmed here. We can never be in any doubt that Petruchio intends to be master of what he owns, and he is prepared to take on a role and work hard to achieve his aims. He is extremely single-minded, and does not waver from his purpose. Not once does he admit that Katherina has her own point of view.

But what does he want? His ambitions are actually quite small, and, **ironically**, at odds with the swashbuckling persona he assumes for much of the play: he declares that he values domestic peace and harmony. All the noise and chaos he causes are intended to secure a quiet life at home. So how does he ensure that he achieves this? Partly by being a fine actor and doggedly and consistently asserting that everything is the opposite of what it seems, but mainly because he possesses a will stronger than anyone else's. The other (male) characters also collude with and assist Petruchio, who is undoubtedly the most masculine and dominant male: he is cock of the walk. There are lines that suggest the master is teacher and educator, but there are also lines that suggest brute force and an uncompromising desire to dominate ruthlessly. Undoubtedly, his educational methods are harsh. His violent tendencies are all directed at his subordinates, and his abuse of those who serve him is intended to remind his wife that she may be next on the list. And if Petruchio does not actually resort to beating his wife, she certainly suffers physically while in his care. The neglect and disinterest of her father's house are replaced by deprivation: no food, no sleep, left in the mire under her horse, and no new clothes or kisses. Petruchio forces his wife to give up her voice by asserting his own right to speak and define the world as he sees it. It becomes clear that his unnatural and eccentric behaviour is licensed while Katherina's is not. We are encouraged to believe that Petruchio is using his role as 'mad-brain rudesby' (III.2.10) to re-educate his wife. At the end of the play we know that Hortensio and Lucentio will need to join Petruchio's taming-school if they are to enjoy peaceful marriages with their wives.

Is Petruchio a playful suitor or misogynist bully? It depends upon whether or not we feel that Katherina has gained or lost by meeting and marrying him. Petruchio's **soliloquies** do not hint at much affection, although at the end of the play we can see that he is satisfied with the wife he has moulded and subdued. The line, 'Why, there's a wench! Come on, and kiss me, Kate' (V.2.181) suggests approval. We might feel that the kisses in the play chart the hero's increasing pleasure in his creation. At the wedding ceremony Petruchio kisses Katherina in order to humiliate her; then at the end of Act IV, he uses a public kiss in the street to test her obedience. Finally in V.2 he rewards Kate – and himself – for her obedience by kissing her prior to the consummation of the marriage. Some see this kiss, and the line quoted above as proof that Petruchio has really been seeking a companionate marriage (although we must not forget that a happy marriage depends upon female submission in this play). *The Taming of the Shrew* clearly demonstrates the importance of female behaviour for a man's reputation: the hawking **imagery** underlines this point. In the closing moments we will certainly view Lucentio and Hortensio as lesser men because they cannot rule their wives. Unlike Petruchio, they do not possess the energy and wit to tame their shrews. Their reputations have suffered, while his has prospered.

KATHERINA

Kate can be seen as a prototype for Shakespeare's energetic, licensed female talkers, Beatrice (*Much Ado About Nothing*) and Paulina (*The Winter's Tale*). However, many feel that the heroine's voice is never given the credit it deserves in this early play. It is possible to argue that Katherina is both defined and destroyed by the male tongue. Her early utterances reflect her reputation as a scold, but the male characters exaggerate her shrewishness. She says less than half as much as Petruchio and her longest and most compelling speech is made – **ironically** – after she has been tamed and given up her distinctive female voice. Prior to this speech, the men have dealt with Katherina by ignoring or contradicting her. Petruchio silences her by being more shrew than she. At the end of the play it is hard to resist the conclusion that Kate is only allowed to deliver her lecture because it has been endorsed by and will please a man. Essentially, Kate has a stereotypical role to play out, one which would have been familiar to the Elizabethan audience from folklore and ballads: she is the scold who must be punished for her waywardness. The treatment she receives bears some resemblance to the traditional methods used to shame shrewish females: the scold's bridle and the ducking stool, both of which were intended to humiliate the scold physically and publicly. Although Petruchio does not resort to the crude physical violence of these methods, he certainly threatens to cuff and restrain Kate.

If Kate is a stereotype, does her character develop? In more positive readings of the play, some critics suggest that she is liberated by Petruchio, who frees her to grow into a contented wife, with a useful role to play outside her father's house. Thus it can be argued that she benefits from the rather brutal education she is forced to endure. Some critics note Katherina's insistence on erotic and emotional pleasure in her final speech, in which she declares that women should submit to their husbands because they work hard to keep their wives 'secure and safe' at home (V.2.152). Are we to assume that she has finally understood the point of being ruled by men?. Her lines towards the end of her lecture suggest she has 'seen the light' and accepted patriarchy's rules (see V.2.170–4).

These lines hint at a change of mind. It is possible to argue that Katherina's style and tone indicate that she has 'grown' and changed. In V.2 she speaks eloquently, forcefully and gracefully, with a measured tone that contrasts sharply with her outbursts in Acts I and II. During Act IV, her combative wit becomes more playful, as we see from her exchanges with Petruchio about the sun and moon in IV.5. Perhaps her quick-wittedness, once employed to snarl and sneer at her unwanted suitor, is now utilised to entertain a husband she has accepted gratefully.

It is possible that these comments are too generous, and do not allow for the outrage that might be felt when watching the heroine being humiliated. Modern audiences are likely to feel that Kate has some cause for her early discontent and shrewishness: the Paduan males are puny, her sister is sanctimonious, and her father mercantile and cold. No-one listens to her. Later she has every right to be outraged by Petruchio's treatment of her, from the wooing scene onwards. A modern audience might also feel that Kate is diminished by the events of the play. Rather than grow, perhaps she is obliterated. The Katherina who speaks at the end of the play seems to possess a masculine view of the world, as if a new persona has been unconvincingly grafted on to the female stereotype by the playwright, who is not really concerned with the consistency of his heroine's characterisation. Katherina becomes the ideal Kate outlined by Petruchio in II.1. Are we then to view her as a figure intended to satisfy a male wish-fulfilment fantasy? As Katherina goes from making demands to following instructions, many would argue that she becomes an increasingly powerless figure: her transformation negates rather than confirms the value of the female. As the title of the play suggests; the taming is more important than the shrew.

It is briefly worth considering Kate's looks, which are not so important to the drama as her scolding tongue, but significant nonetheless. Is the shrew ugly or fair, like her sister? Outward appearances are consistently deceptive in this play, in which men judge women according to their physical attributes and silence. Critics are divided about whether or not Kate's looks are as abhorrent as her voice. There are conflicting descriptions in I.2; the heroine is 'ill-favour'd (I.2.59) early in the scene, becoming 'young and beauteous' (I.2.85) as

Hortensio realises that Petruchio will take her on. Petruchio then complicates matters by seeming to praise Katherina's appearance in II.1:

> Why does the world report that Kate doth limp?
> O slanderous world! Kate like the hazel-twig
> Is straight and slender, and as brown in hue
> As hazel-nuts and sweeter than the kernels (II.1.246–9)

He adds that her 'beauty … doth make me like thee well' (II.1.267). However, all these words are uttered in a scene in which Petruchio often asserts the opposite of what he knows to be true. Is this another example of the hero taunting the heroine? If his praise is **ironic**, then Katherina looks even more like a victim.

Katherina's relationship with the other female characters in the play is important. Unlike Shakespeare's other heroines of comedy, Kate has no female friend or confidante: her isolation perhaps shows us how at odds she is with society. Both before and after her taming, she seems to remain antagonistic towards other women. Some critics have suggested that she redirects the venom she displayed towards Bianca in Act II at the Widow in the final scene. Neither her sister nor the Widow respond to her final speech; the male characters are alone when they celebrate the taming of the shrew. Has Kate turned on her 'sisters' in a different way? Can we view her as an enemy of her own sex, having been misled into believing that she was an enemy to men?

BIANCA

Bianca's characterisation is sketchy but intriguing. To begin with she seems to be as much a female stereotype as her sister: she is the silent, obedient maiden whom suitors flock to worship. But if Shakespeare seems to insist that the scold can be brought into line in the taming plot, the opposite is true in the subplot. From early on the playwright hints that Bianca will please herself, although she initially appears to be a victim. Like Katherina, she is mewed up and thwarted at home; but this female rebels by seeming to conform. By cultivating a silent and demure exterior, Bianca dupes others. It is noticeable that she says more, and speaks more assertively as the play progresses, providing a point of contrast with her sister, who is becoming less vocal. Bianca's submissive outward appearance gives her some power: she is able to choose a husband by deceiving her father. There is a good deal of **irony** in her characterisation. Is she the real shrew in this play, far more dangerous than her railing, brawling sister? Because Bianca is unmasked as a shrew, there is no real **closure** at the end of Act V. One scold is silenced, but the other has gained what she wanted, and her reign has just begun.

BAPTISTA

Baptista Minola is a conventional Elizabethan patriarch. He is attached to at least one of his daughters, but views both as objects to be bartered on the marriage market. The clever father keeps Bianca in reserve while he follows the custom of marrying off his eldest daughter first; this is canny: it will raise her price, suggested by the fact that Bianca gains suitors as the play progresses. Baptista uses Bianca's suitors to find a husband for his difficult daughter; thus saving him the troublesome task of locating a man to take Katherina on. Many critics comment on his lack of concern for Kate, and consider the Minolas dysfunctional. Generally, Baptista disregards his eldest daughter's feelings, although he shows some sympathy for her on her wedding day when Petruchio is late. However, this remark, and his rather lame insistence that Petruchio must win his daughter's love (see II.1.128–9) are unconvincing. Essentially, Baptista allows the pirate to make off with Kate because, as Gremio and Hortensio recognise, he wants to be rid of her. It seems just and appropriate, then, that his conniving younger daughter gets the better of him. This is **ironic**, because Baptista puts more energy, effort and guile into disposing of his 'treasure' (II.1.32). He plays the suitors off against one another, looking for the most advantageous match, simultaneously proving himself to be as careless of his younger daughter's feelings as he was of the elder's. His lines in IV.4 show this. Here he speaks brazenly of knowing Bianca's heart and mind: we know he does not. Ultimately, however, the father is not punished for his mercantile approach to matrimony. He is humiliated by Lucentio, Tranio and Bianca, but the former is an eminently suitable match, socially and financially: he is the kind of son-in-law Baptista would have chosen. Because this is a comedy, the deception and self-delusion of the father do not lead to tragedy, as they will in *King Lear* (1605) and *The Winter's Tale* (1611).

THE SUITORS

LUCENTIO

Lucentio is presented as the young Elizabethan gallant, idealistic but rather ridiculous in his romantic aspirations. He is the opposite of Petruchio, and unlike the more vigorous wooer, requires some education himself if he is to achieve a happy marriage, his goal from the first scene in which he appears. Unlike the self-sufficient protagonist, Lucentio has to rely on others to organise his wooing and wedding, hinting at the fact that he will be duped by Bianca. In the end, like Hortensio, he is no match for the duplicitous female he is united with, in spite of the fact that he too has acted the role of deceiver. Lucentio is a benign, comic figure, whose courtly approach and classical allusions are undermined and ridiculed by the robust action and outcome of the play.

HORTENSIO

Hortensio provides another point of comparison with Petruchio, the successful woman-tamer, and Lucentio, the courtly lover. He lacks the masculine vigour of the former and the romantic conviction of the latter, although he professes to be very much in love with Bianca in Act I (see I.2.173–4). Hortensio's lack of success with women makes him a source of comedy; rejected by Bianca, he is physically abused by Katherina and bested by his Widow. He is an impotent figure, no match for the other men or women in the play. Like Lucentio, he has a lot to learn. Hortensio's attitude to marriage highlights the social and financial concerns of the Elizabethan male. He declares he will no longer court Bianca when he discovers she has looked at another man and settles for a wealthy widow instead. Hortensio's admiring responses to Petruchio's taming methods, and his assistance in the subjection of Kate in IV.3 demonstrate the superior attitude of men towards women in this play. But this male is not assertive enough to capitalise on the lesson he is presented with.

GREMIO

Gremio's characterisation is inspired by the pantaloon from Italian ***commedia dell'arte***, in which wealthy old buffoons unsuccessfully and foolishly court young women. Gremio adds to our understanding of the masculine values that dominate this play, showing a traditional male abhorrence of the scold. He frequently makes derogatory comments about Kate, and serves as another comic foil in the subplot, as a rival to Hortensio and Lucentio. After the wedding of Katherina and Petruchio his role is not significant, although he continues to comment on the action, adding to our understanding of characters and events (particularly the Kate–Petruchio match) and to the confusion in the scene of unmasking that occurs in Act IV. His forced resignation from the battlefield of love is accepted with good grace, and he is content to obtain a hearty meal instead. Thus we might feel that his unsuccessful wooing, like Hortensio's, undermines the romantic Lucentio's approach.

THE SERVANTS

As is often the case in Elizabethan and Jacobean drama, the servants in *The Taming of the Shrew* are lively, resourceful figures, as quick-witted as their masters (often more so). They assist with the matrimonial plans and intrigues, taking on roles in order to participate in the action. However, in each case, the servant's subversive or anarchic potential is contained.

TRANIO

Tranio is the most important servant in the play. Without his clever plotting, Lucentio would not 'achieve' (I.1.156) fair Bianca. He has a persuasive tongue and is able to transform himself at will. Tranio seems to be well-educated, as his classical allusions in I.1 show: he easily takes on his master's role and language. He is accepted and adept in his disguise, becoming increasingly active as he pursues his plots. At times he seems to be stage-managing the action of the subplot, most notably when he sets up his master's wedding and involves the Pedant in their affairs. However, we have to remember that Tranio is at all times serving Lucentio's ends; he is not punished for assuming the role of a wealthy gentleman because, essentially, he has always maintained his role as servant. As in *Twelfth Night*, the role-reversal is licensed and temporary. Tranio is put back in his place firmly in Act V after the high-jinks are over, and has never really been a threat to the hierarchy, although he has caused the older male characters some disquiet. He speaks – as Katherina caused the older male characters some disquiet. He speaks – as Katherina learns to – when called upon to do so.

Shakespeare is having fun with Tranio, as he is with Biondello, who plays the role of cheeky page. This character is a helpful messenger. His lively descriptions of the wedding and quick-witted improvisations add to the comedy of the play. Like Tranio, he resembles his comic ancestors from ***commedia dell'arte*** and the servants in the sources Shakespeare used (see Structure).

Grumio

Grumio is most important as a foil for Petruchio, although he makes astute remarks about other characters too (most notably Gremio). He is a clownish figure, rather like a licensed court jester, who tells the truth about and to his master, affording us another view of the protagonist's character. Grumio alerts us to Petruchio's shrewish tendencies and potential for violence, thereby helping to set up the verbal combat that occurs during the 'courtship' of Katherina. This servant shares his master's verbal dexterity, sharp wits, and ability to argue his listener into submission. His 'backchat' in I.2 might be seen as subversive, but like Tranio, Grumio faithfully assists in his master's schemes. Following Petruchio's example and instructions he taunts Katherina with food in Act IV, playing his part in the taming. This is not unexpected; at the wedding he was 'caparisoned like the horse', 'a very monster in apparel' (III.2.63–8). Like Biondello, Grumio is a source of verbal comedy. In IV.1 he describes offstage events in a colourful way. This narrative of the journey home is vivid and amusing. His treatment of Curtis mirrors and anticipates Petruchio's approach to his goods and chattels, demonstrating that Katherina will be brought into line. The 'pecking order' is made clear in IV.1. Interestingly, Grumio gets away with far more than Katherina is ever allowed to: his cheek is tolerated.

Christopher sly

Sly's situation parallels Katherina's: he is transformed. However, his is a temporary metamorphosis, like Tranio's. Like Lucentio's clever servant, he enjoys being allowed to take on a new social identity and lording it in a different class, although he has more difficulty adapting to his changed role. Perhaps his struggle foreshadows Katherina's. Certainly his initial bewilderment in Scene 2 of the **Induction** mirrors her dazed reactions to Petruchio in Act IV. Sly's energetic speeches anticipate Katherina's shrewish voice of Acts I and II and he is a source of verbal and visual **comedy**, ridiculous but entertaining as he calls for a pot of ale in his luxurious and elegant surroundings.

Sly is perhaps the only truly realistic character in *The Taming of the Shrew*. Critics have commented on the fact that Shakespeare deliberately casts him as a Warwickshire man, and his down-to-earth style is the opposite of the romantic and more artificial, courtly tones of Lucentio and the Lord. Sly is a man of the street and the tavern. Perhaps his vigour foreshadows Petruchio, whom some critics also characterise as true to life (see comments in Critical History). Sly's urgent desire to bed his 'wife' is human and unromantic, and leads the way for the unromantic and **farcical** comedy that is presented for his entertainment. His boredom with the play seems proof of his earthy vitality. Like Petruchio, he 'would fain be doing' (II.1.74).

THEMES

ROMANCE & MARRIAGE

Some critics suggest that we must view *The Shrew* as a romantic **comedy**; others believe there is little romance in this knockabout **farce** concerning the war between the sexes. The play ends with the traditional gathering of married couples, but their progress towards the altar has been characterised by tricks, ruses and brute force. It can be argued that the action of the taming plot systematically undermines the romantic impulses and gestures that we see enacted in the Bianca subplot. Through his portrayal of Kate and Petruchio Shakespeare perhaps rejects the notions of courtly love the naïve Lucentio espouses.

Matrimony is clearly the chief concern of all the characters in this play, but with the exception of Lucentio, none of the characters appears to adopt a genuinely romantic approach to wooing and wedding a suitable partner. Baptista plays 'a merchant's part' (II.1.319) throughout. Hortensio and Gremio, ostensibly romantic wooers drawn by Bianca's beauty, are actually engaged in a masculine competition, which involves providing a 'good deal' for her father and hiring suitable schoolmasters. When Tranio enters the field in disguise, they are concerned because he appears to be a very wealthy young gentleman, and is therefore a better prospect. Hortensio reveals his true colours when he settles for a wealthy 'lusty widow' (IV.2.50). Lucentio's romantic musings would lead nowhere without Tranio's practical scheming. Worshipping from afar simply will not do; he won't 'achieve' (I.1.156) the maid this way. When he does 'achieve' her, Lucentio finds that Bianca is not the goddess of maidenly modesty and sobriety he took her for. Lucentio's values are foolish: he has a faulty approach to love and marriage. The careers of Hortensio and Lucentio suggest that matrimony is as hazardous as business. This idea is summed up by Baptista when he refers to the way in which he has to 'venture madly on a desperate mart' in his quest to marry Bianca off to the highest bidder (II.1.320).

The anti-romantic Petruchio is presented as a 'winner' (V.2.188), confirming that wooing is a competition. Pursuing the female is not the only challenge; establishing the way in which a happy marriage will work is also a contest. This is the focus of the main plot. Petruchio's mercantile approach, which fits in with the 'merchant's part' his father-in-law plays, is established within minutes of his arrival on stage. During the course of the play his wealth increases dramatically as he takes on and tames his bride. Is this a brutal or realistic view of the way marriages operated during the Renaissance? In later plays Shakespeare seems to insist that mutual affection is a vital part of a good match, although he also suggests that a down-to-earth approach is necessary; his heroes who do not look beyond appearances often find themselves in trouble. In *The Shrew* the message seems to be that a happy marriage depends first and foremost on female subordination, a model that we find unpalatable today. But critics have argued that Kate's final speech does not just show the importance of female submission. Some argue that she outlines the idea that men and women have duties to one another. While the woman lies 'warm at home, secure and safe', her mate goes out into the world, 'To painful labour by both sea and land'. Because he works for her 'maintenance' the woman owes her husband 'love, fair looks, and true obedience; / Too little payment for so great a debt' (V.2.149–55). It seems that both sexes have distinct roles in marriage. However, Kate uses language that makes some commentators uneasy; she speaks of 'payment', suggesting that the traffic is perhaps still one way, as it was when Baptista played Bianca's suitors off against one another earlier in the play. The dismay Lucentio displays when he realises his wife is not a dove shows that he has made a bad bargain. We cannot avoid the conclusion that the best kind of woman to marry is silent, or one whose tongue is used to serve and support men. Bianca is so attractive initially because she is quiet; when she voices her opinions in Act V she becomes troublesome. Conversely, Kate is licensed to talk at the end of the play because she speaks on cue, when she is asked to do so. She is no longer assertive and does not use her tongue to make demands any more.

Some critics have argued that this play represents an anachronistic view of marriage, that was already out-of-date at the time the play was first performed; others remain convinced that the message the play offers of the desirability of wife-taming was to be taken seriously. Katherina's offer to place her hand beneath her husband's foot was a gesture inspired by a part of the wedding ceremony that had been prohibited forty years before Shakespeare wrote *The Shrew*. And it is true that marriage was an institution being redefined at the end of the sixteenth century. A number of Elizabethan commentators suggested that wives should be seen as joint governors in the household, who should not be beaten. At the same time domestic violence was not illegal, and many writers of books and homilies which offered advice on how to conduct oneself in marriage held that it was legitimate to use force if it was necessary for maintaining right supremacy. Historians have proved that domestic violence was widespread. And it is was often a source of comedy in ballads and puppet shows during this period, as well as a suitable subject for humour on the stage. Because this play is a **comedy**, and the beatings that occur are intended to make us laugh, it seems that the play might be seen as subscribing to 'old' rather than new views about matrimony. However, the fact that Petruchio, as one critic puts it, 'creates chaos in the central locations of marriage [the dining table and the bed]' and then resolves this disorder without resorting to his fists (although he does of course beat his servants) suggests that the protagonist is not entirely unenlightened. But he has a long way to go before he becomes the Elizabethan equivalent of a 'new man'.

MONEY & SOCIETY

Money is a prerequisite for marriage – wise fathers and wooers think of little else. Petruchio is attracted to Kate solely because of her dowry; if he does, as some critics feel, find that he loves her, then this is a bonus. He states clearly that money alone would be enough: 'I come to wive it wealthily in Padua, / If wealthily, then happily in Padua' (I.2.74–5). Petruchio is rewarded for taming his wife with a second dowry, also gaining financially as a result of the wager in Act V. Lucentio is an acceptable son-in-law in spite of his subterfuge: he is the son of a wealthy gentleman. Significantly, the women have no part in the financial dealings that concern their futures. This play suggests patriarchy is alive and well.

We see an acquisitive middle class and very masculine society in *The Taming of the Shrew*. It is run along hierarchical lines, from the **Induction** onwards. The Lord toys with his social inferior Sly for amusement, and his pursuits (hunting) are those of a gentleman. His servants obey him absolutely. Those who are allowed to usurp the positions of their betters in the subplot (Tranio, Biondello) are eventually returned to their roles, just as Bartholomew the page and Sly will probably return to a more mundane reality when the dream is over (although there is no **epilogue** to show that this is what the dramatist intended). Similarly, Kate will learn what role she should play and take her place in the hierarchy accordingly. Social status and middle-class life are evoked by references to possessions and leisure pursuits; boots, clothes, books, instruments, dogs, horses, hawks are all signs of social standing. Women are **symbols** of men's power, or lack of it. Baptista has one marriageable daughter and a shrew, who is presented as worthless until she is tamed. Hortensio and Gremio are laughable figures because they fail to 'achieve' the woman of their dreams. Petruchio's obedient Kate increases his prestige. Altogether, this is a play about masculine assertiveness, masculine negotiations and game-playing (see the repeated references to betting and card games), and masculine ideals.

DECEPTION

The theme of deception can be linked to illusion and transformation; these ideas are woven seamlessly together in *The Shrew*. There is much deceit in the play, creating numerous examples of **dramatic irony**. Disguises are used to achieve transformations in character and circumstances. In the Induction the Lord uses both illusion and reality to convince Sly that he is a nobleman, his fortunes transformed. Concrete details – pictures, music, food, clothes and a 'wife' – all persuade the tinker that he is a lord. But we know that he will come down to earth with a bump when the real Lord becomes bored with acting out his fantasy. Some would argue that the presence of the fake lord (Sly) on stage during the main play means that we should understand that Petruchio's taming of his wife is simply a temporary 'wonder' (V.2.190), like the beggar's changed circumstances. Others argue that this reading of V.2 is hard to sustain because there is no final framing scene or **epilogue** involving Sly after the taming story is finished. By this point we will – probably – have forgotten the artful theatrical induction that introduced the action; so, as a number of critics observe, a strong illusion of reality surrounds Kate's final speech. It is difficult *not* to believe in her transformation. We will remain more convinced by her 'act' (if act it is) as an obedient wife than Sly's performance as a lord.

The differences between appearances and reality established in the Induction are highlighted by the use of disguises in the plot and subplot. Tranio and Lucentio set up a hoax as elaborate as the Lord's, and Biondello is brought in, like Bartholomew, to help carry out the scheme. This subterfuge is intended to provide Lucentio with a new role; that of husband to the divine Bianca. We realise that Lucentio is intent on presenting himself as a bold adventurer (rather like Petruchio) when he deceives Biondello with a story of his having to assume a disguise because he has 'kill'd a man' (I.1.231). His fantasies don't stop there, and he is punished for not looking beyond Bianca's appearance. As is frequently the case in *The Shrew*, it is **ironic** that the deceiver is deceived. Hortensio's disguise leads to failure of another kind. He congratulates himself for discovering that Bianca is courting 'Cambio', but does not look closely enough at his Widow. Petruchio, meanwhile, has been busy acting out the role of eccentric wife-tamer in order to create a new reality for himself as a married man. He uses his disguise to effect what he hopes will be a lasting transformation in his wife. As in the Induction, the dominant male is attempting to change another character's understanding of and response to the circumstances she finds herself in. But is Petruchio really in disguise? The protagonist is consistently upfront about his motives and does not deceive anybody, least of all Kate, about his intentions. Until the last act of the play, many doubt that he will be able to carry his project off. It is ironic that the one character whose behaviour is considered odd is proved to have been telling the truth all along. Petruchio does, however, use his storytelling and acting powers to transform his wife. Bianca is just as successful at acting as he, and she too gets what she wants. These two wily creatures prove that power can be gained by playing a role with your eyes open, if you have enough determination, and a clear understanding of those you seek to influence.

IMAGERY

Although patterns of **imagery** are not used so extensively and densely in *The Taming of the Shrew* as they are in Shakespeare's later works, an analysis of the **figurative language** helps to inform our understanding of characters, events and themes.

THE DEVIL

On several occasions Kate's shrewish disposition is commented on, particularly in the early scenes of the play. Images of hell are invoked to demonstrate the men's abhorrence of her wayward tongue and behaviour; and they help to establish the idea that many of the male characters are rather frightened of the heroine. This comes across clearly in Gremio's utterances in Act I, particularly his line, 'From all such devils, good Lord, deliver us!' (I.1.66). Kate is 'this fiend of hell' (I.1.88), fit only to 'go to the devil's dam' (I.1.105). Gremio wonders whether he and Hortensio will be able to light on 'any man [who] is so very a fool as to be married to hell' (I.1.124–5). Even her father refers to Kate as a 'hilding of a devilish spirit' (II.1.26). All these references establish the scold's unnatural and inhuman persona. Kate lives up to her diabolical reputation when she breaks the lute over Hortensio's head, showing, as he suggests, a 'most impatient devilish spirit' (II.1.151). Her actions and the men's words seem to fit together. Or do they? Some critics suggest that the exaggeration of these invocations of devilry are absurd; surely the worst we can accuse Kate of is possessing a bad temper? It is significant that Petruchio disregards all the warnings he receives about uniting himself in matrimony with 'hell'. After the episode with the lute he announces boldly that he loves her 'ten times more than e'er I did' (II.1.161), effectively undermining the legitimacy of the imagery the other male characters use. To be sure, he is exaggerating as much as they are, but Petruchio shows his superior masculinity when he proves that he is willing and ready to do battle with the forces of evil. The Paduans are the fools, not Petruchio. The linking of shrews and hell was traditional during the period in which the play was written; the creatures were commonly associated with dark, sinister forces. The 'little din' (I.2.198) that the shrew Kate makes is intended to add to her characterisation (and some would say vilification) as a scold; shrews were thought to be noisy, aggressive and voracious little beasts.

ANIMALS, HUNTING & HAWKING

There are many images of animals, hunting and hawking throughout the play. All these references are intended to evoke the natural order, the hierarchy that decreed that women were inferior to men. Animal imagery informs our understanding of Petruchio's wife-taming methods too. At the time the play was written falconry was an expensive and laborious pursuit, not exclusively the preserve of the aristocracy, but certainly associated with it: thus Petruchio is presented as the most 'worthy' character in the main play. He has the skill to tame his wife, just as the aristocrat developed the skill to tame his hawk.

In the first scene of the **Induction**, set in a natural environment, the Lord returns from hunting, discussing the merits of his hounds. It seems that everything is in order here; the hierarchy of the First and Second Huntsman and their polite obedience, the dogs' fine efforts out in the field, the Lord in command. This is the harmony that Petruchio will work hard to achieve in his own household. Like the Lord, the protagonist might be considered a willing and determined huntsman (the Lord intends hunting again the following day). Petruchio comes to Padua to 'wive it wealthily' (I.2.74). At the end of the play Tranio will refer explicitly to Petruchio's achievements as a 'hunter' (V.2.52–6) who has succeeded in turning his 'wildcat' (I.2.195) wife into a 'slow-wing'd turtle

[dove]' (II.1.207). The hawking **motif** that runs through the play is established early when Petruchio and Katherina meet for the first time. Kate is asked whether 'a buzzard' should 'take thee?' (II.1.207). Outlining his scheme to achieve domestic dominion Petruchio is quite clear about his intentions:

> My falcon now is sharp and passing empty,
> And till she stoop she must not be full-gorg'd,
> For then she never looks upon her lure.
> Another way I have to man my haggard,
> To make her come and know her keeper's call,
> That is, to watch her …
> She ate no meat today, nor none shall eat;
> Last night she slept not, nor tonight she shall not. (IV.1.177–85)

In this way he hopes to 'curb' his wife's 'mad and headstrong humour' (IV.1.196). His methods exactly match those used by a gentleman training his hawk. We might feel that a hawk is most natural when it is a 'haggard' (wild), but the imagery forces us to understand that a husband's successful 'reign' depends upon showing his wife that she must 'know her keeper's call'. The hawk must not be in control of its master. The final scene demonstrates this most clearly.

Petruchio's use of his horses adds to our impression of him as successful hunter and shrew-tamer. The ailing beast he rides to his wedding humiliates Kate as much as his clothes (the long description of it by Biondello suggests its importance). On the way home Katherina's horse stumbles, 'and she under her horse … in how miry a place' (IV.1.66–8). Grumio adds the telling detail, 'how she was bemoiled'. It could be argued that the horse has punished the shrew for her attempted defiance at the end of Act III, when she stamped her feet and declared she would not leave until after the feast. When Kate comes off in the mire, and Petruchio leaves her there, we know she is floundering: the animal-tamer will have his way. Some critics feel that it is significant that Kate finally submits to her husband in the open air, on the journey back to Padua: has she finally demonstrated that she is 'at one' with nature and the hierarchy? In the closing scene there are images that suggest that the natural order has been achieved in one marriage, but subverted in two others, causing grief. Bianca reproves Petruchio when she says, 'Am I your bird? I mean to shift my bush, / and then pursue me as you draw your bow' (V.2.46–7). The implication of these lines is that Petruchio may have tamed *his* 'bird', but Bianca remains at liberty and may 'shift' her 'bush' and act as she pleases. However, harmony has been restored elsewhere. Tranio has returned to his proper station in life, signalled by his rueful statement, 'O sir, Lucentio slipp'd me like his greyhound, / Which runs himself, and catches for his master' (V.2.52–3). His acting out the role of gentleman has never really been a threat to the natural order. The banter continues with further animal imagery. **Ironically**, the Paduans still believe that Petruchio's wife is unruly: ''Tis thought your deer does hold you at a bay' (V.2.56) says Tranio. But the suspense is soon over and Petruchio shows that he does not have 'the veriest shrew of all' (V.2.64). The wager is very much like a modern bet on horses or dogs. Petruchio says that he'll venture 'twenty times so much upon my wife' as he would on 'my hawk or hound' (V.2.72–3). It comes as no surprise when the most daring gamester wins and Katherina performs, as P.J. Gabriner suggests, rather like a 'trained bear' (see Critical History).

EDUCATION

References to teaching and learning add to our understanding of Petruchio's wife-taming methods, and perhaps indicate that we should see the protagonist in a slightly more favourable light than some commentators suggest. But it is not just Katherina who is educated; other characters learn lessons in the course of the play. When he first arrives in Padua we are told that Lucentio has come to 'institute / A course of learning and ingenious studies' (I.1.8–9). This is appropriate for a young gentleman of his status. However, he swiftly throws off all thoughts of 'sweet philosophy' (I.1.28) when he sees Bianca. Lucentio then uses education to pursue his amorous aims, taking on the role of schoolmaster as he attempts to woo Bianca. We swiftly realise he is the one in need of teaching. Shakespeare perhaps undermines traditional ideas about the value of book-learning in his portrayal of this young lover. For all his reading, Lucentio not only needs the assistance of the more practical Tranio to win his fair lady, but he also fails to look beyond her beautiful, mute exterior. Lucentio's use of Ovid's 'The Art of Loving' further undermines him. Brian Morris, editor of the Arden edition of *The*

Taming of the Shrew says that this book is 'a witty, cynical textbook for seducers', 'anything but a manual for romantic lovers'. That Lucentio fails to notice this suggests his naïveté. **Ironically**, the other naïve male suitor, Hortensio, also takes on the role of schoolmaster. The fact that Baptista places such a high value on his favourite daughter's education hints at the delight and admiration he will feel at the end of the play when he learns that his son-in-law Petruchio has succeeded in 'educating' his other daughter Katherina.

Petruchio's approach is altogether more down to earth. His experience of the world, not the university, will help him in his 'taming-school' (IV.2.54). The hero has 'heard lions roar', 'heard the sea, puff'd up with winds', 'heard great ordnance in the field / And heaven's artillery thunder in the skies' (I.2.199–203). Thus he is well prepared to take on and silence 'a woman's tongue' (I.2.206). When Gremio says that he comes from the wedding ceremony 'As willingly as e'er I came from school', we get a hint that Petruchio's educational methods, while rather perplexing, are already efficacious. By the end of the play the male characters have realised this. Hortensio says that Petruchio has 'taught' him to be 'untoward' if his Widow 'be froward' (IV.5.77–8) Petruchio has proved the truth of a moral lesson: that peace and harmony in marriage depend upon wifely submission.

FOOD & CLOTHING

Allusions to food and clothing suggest that this is a play very much concerned with the material world. This fits in with the portrayal of marriage as a business venture (see Themes). References to clothes also help the dramatist explore ideas about appearance and reality. In the **Induction**, Sly is fooled by his own and others' outward appearances. When he is put in 'a costly suit' (Ind.1.57) and presented with a 'wife' (a page in disguise) he gradually becomes convinced that he is a lord. This suggests just how powerful attractive outward appearances can be. In the subplot disguises abound. Ironically, no-one looks beyond Bianca's pleasing exterior; the 'sweet beauty in her face' (I.1.167) conceals a strong will. For a long time Tranio fools everyone too, causing Gremio and Hortensio, as well as the real Vincentio and Baptista, a good deal of worry before he is unmasked as an impostor. While his unmasking is comic, and leads to the restoration of order, Bianca's unmasking is more problematic for those she has deceived.

Petruchio's use of a 'disguise' is as calculated as the other characters'. It is both comic and serious. He takes on the role of 'mad-brain rudesby' (III.2.10). When he arrives at the wedding 'mean apparell'd' (III.2.71) he presents an extraordinary picture, which never fails to raise a laugh on stage. He defends his peculiar attire thus; 'To me she's married, not unto my clothes' (III.2.115). This line suggests that he, unlike Lucentio and Hortensio, has the wit to look beyond appearances. But his costume serves another purpose too; he is mocking his bride by going against accepted customs of dress, demonstrating to her the importance of complying with conventions. For the same reason he rejects the tailor's gown in IV.3. Katherina has not yet submitted to him, so she doesn't deserve new clothes. When she has a new persona, she gets her cap and gown, **symbols** of her status as obedient married woman. At the end of the play Kate shows that she has conformed by throwing her cap on the ground when her husband asks her to.

The numerous references to food serve a number of purposes. The delights of a good feast are established in the Induction when Sly is plied with all manner of delicacies. He betrays his class origins by calling for 'a pot o' th' smallest ale' (Ind.2.76), but we see the importance of appetite. We also learn in the Induction that Sly is presented with a play because it is thought that this will drive away 'the melancholy' (Ind.2.133). Food and good mental health are linked in the main action of the play. Katherina is deprived of food and not allowed to participate in a wedding feast until she has emerged from her diseased state as shrew. Petruchio tells her that he will not let her touch the meat that has been prepared because 'it engenders choler, planteth anger' (IV.1.158). Her submission is the source of celebration in the final scene, when the delayed festivities take place. A cheerful mood is established when Lucentio calls on the guests to 'chat as well as eat' (V.2.11). It is intended that the banquet will 'close our stomachs up / After our great good cheer' (V.2.9–10). These lines indicate that the quarrelling is over. This is because Kate, whose name was a source of puns (Kate-cake), is now palatable. Women are further linked to food when Gremio says 'My cake is dough' (V.1.128), recognising that his chances of marrying Bianca have been swept away. Wisely, he settles for his share of the feast instead. However, we know the man who got the cake will not find her as delicious in the eating as he expected.

Language & style

The Taming of the Shrew is written in prose and **blank verse** (unrhymed iambic pentameter), which Shakespeare uses flexibly. Prose was traditionally used by low or comic characters and the dramatist follows this convention to an extent; Sly, Grumio, Biondello and Curtis habitually converse in prose, often to great comic effect (see Biondello's description of Petruchio's arrival in Act III and Grumio's account of the journey to Petruchio's house in Act IV for good examples of entertaining, swift-moving prose). Prose is employed to draw social distinctions. However, the servants occasionally speak in verse, depending upon the effect that Shakespeare wishes to achieve; for example, Grumio delivers a rather clumsy rhyming couplet in I.2.128–9, neatly encapsulating the problem Petruchio faces when he agrees to woo Kate ('Katherine the curst, / A title for a maid of all titles the worst'). The servants make effective use of **puns**, as befits their roles as comic foils (see Grumio's exchange with Petruchio at the opening of I.2). Sly shifts sharply from prose to verse while under the Lord's influence in the second scene of the **Induction**, suggesting the power of transformation. The effect is again comic; the idea of a drunken tinker adopting the polite and formal mode of his social superiors makes us laugh. It is noticeable, however, that Sly finds it hard to speak this language consistently; at line 126 in the same scene he returns to his humbler prose. In the subplot Tranio presents an interesting case. Although he is a servant, and of a superior kind to Biondello, he speaks in verse. His understanding and use of classical and literary allusions, typical of the love-lorn Lucentio, mark him out as a bright and witty fellow. We are not surprised that he has none of Sly's difficulty in adopting a new voice; in fact, the measured style he uses when he appears as 'Lucentio' in II.1 is as assured as his earlier speeches in I.1. He certainly convinces Bianca's other suitors that they have cause to worry. Part of Tranio's success must be attributed to his quick-witted ability to use his tongue persuasively: he is able to convince the Pedant that he is in danger and almost gets away with his disguise because the Paduans find him so convincing in the role of gentleman.

Lucentio speaks in a style appropriate to a courtly lover with romantic aspirations, for example his speech with classical allusions in I.1.167–70. The grandiose, mock-heroic and rather stilted style is appropriate to the naïve young man. We know that we should regard his poetic approach as comic when Tranio immediately tries to bring his master down to earth in the lines that follow this speech. Lucentio's style contrasts neatly with the language that we come to associate with Petruchio. As befits the man who wins the day because he is able to 'rail in his rope-tricks' (I.2.110–11), the protagonist's speech is lively and varied, and he has a great deal to say for himself. Petruchio is capable of the heroic (see his description of his adventures in I.2), and of rhetoric (see his speech about his 'household stuff' in III.2). But much of what he says is direct and pithy, devoid of the romantic **imagery** so beloved by Lucentio. He does make classical allusions in I.2 but their effect is comic rather than proof of a romantic disposition (see glossary for I.2).

Petruchio is associated with oaths, threats and abuse, with imagery of hawking and hunting, and with swift and successful word-play. His wooing of Katherina is a devastating example of the latter. In this combat, which proceeds in **stichomythia** (a dialogue carried out in single alternating lines), he makes a number of bawdy puns which show his ability to talk his audience down. We have been prepared for this dialogue by his argument with Grumio in I.2. Petruchio is an effective storyteller, as we see when Baptista returns to the stage after this contest. He constructs a tall story of what has just occurred: 'She hung about my neck, and kiss on kiss / She vied so fast, protesting oath on oath, / That in a twink she won me to her love' (II.1.301–3). This comic and ludicrous exaggeration is typical of Petruchio and his methods of persuasion: he describes things as he would have them and ultimately gets his own way because he is prepared to stick to his version of reality. The breathless energy of Petruchio's wooing style exactly foreshadows his actions later in the play.

The text is full of linguistic competitiveness, appropriate since the play focuses on the war between the sexes. Kate interrogates her sister. Hortensio and Lucentio vie for Bianca's ear and heart. Gremio and

Tranio/'Lucentio' try to outdo each other with descriptions of what they have to offer as suitors. At the wedding there is an altercation when Kate tries to persuade her husband to stay in Padua for the feast. In Act IV, she finds arguing is pointless, because Petruchio either contradicts her or delivers a sermon. The couple continue to scrap about food, clothes and whether the sun is the moon. The increasing absurdity of these 'discussions' is comic, culminating in the scene in which Kate submits (perhaps the most absurd scene of all?). On the road to Padua Katherina meets Vincentio, and at her husband's request greets him as 'Young budding virgin, fair and fresh' (IV.5.36). It seems that she has learned a few verbal tricks from her master; her inappropriate descriptions show that she has given up quarrelling. From now on she will describe and see the world in the way that Petruchio wants her to.

In the final scene Kate demonstrates an even more impressive ability to speak her husband's language when she delivers her speech about the duties wives owe their husbands. This is important. Early in the play we learn that Kate's language and style make her objectionable; now she is allowed to speak at length because she speaks on cue. Her early talk was characterised by forceful, direct, short speeches, full of indignant questions, which nobody wanted to hear. Her final speech is utterly different; formal, measured, full of imagery of war: it hints that her husband has won the battle. It is rhetoric, reminiscent of Petruchio's longer speeches. His triumph is displayed through her rhetorical skill. Kate speaks half as many lines as Petruchio: her linguistic power has never been as great as his, indicating what the outcome of the play will be. We might feel that the lack of **soliloquies** for Kate reveals the masculine bias of the text: the taming is more important than the shrew. Petruchio delivers only two soliloquies, but they are not used to reveal a complex inner life; they are a means by which the audience finds out how he will woo and tame his wife: they are proof of power. His **aside** to Hortensio in IV.3.50 serves the same purpose; it shows us that the hero is in control. Elsewhere asides are used to reveal thoughts and feelings and make subversive jokes. The style and construction of the play, which includes few very long speeches and a lot of fast-moving, witty dialogue, reflect Petruchio's methods and compliment the visual comedy. In Petruchio's case, language *is* power. The exuberance of his verse is a large part of what makes the play so entertaining on stage, and Petruchio the most compelling talker. Silence is important too. The fact that the women are often bystanders suggests that they are less important than the men, and Katherina's dumbfounded silence can certainly indicate powerlessness. But Bianca's silence means something different, hinting that we might consider her sister's silence more closely too. Bianca uses silence to get what she wants: a voice that her husband will be forced to listen to unless he can tame her. What else does her silence mean? Subversion? Wilful wiliness? Duplicity? Does her unmasking as a shrew hint that Katherina may again break out and speak her own language once more?

A final comment on the language of this play. In spite of the Italian names and phrases and Latin quotations that appear, this is a very English play, as the colloquial descriptions of Grumio and Biondello demonstrate. The Italian phrasing adds colour, but the really inspired passages are most definitely English. Comically, Grumio cannot even tell the difference between Latin and Italian, betraying his English roots immediately. The use of Italian and Latin hint at the sources Shakespeare used (see Structure below).

STRUCTURE

A discussion of the sources that Shakespeare used when writing *The Taming of the Shrew* will show just how skilfully his play is constructed. The Bianca subplot is taken from George Gascoigne's comedy *Supposes* (1566), which was essentially a translation of *I Supposti* (1509), an Italian comedy by Ariosto. A 'Suppose', according to Gascoigne's prologue 'is nothing other else but a mystaking or imagination of one thing for another': hence the disguises that we find in *The Shrew*. Italy was often used as a setting for plays of intrigue during this period. Although the subplot follows Gascoigne and Ariosto quite closely, there are differences that suggest that Shakespeare wished to make his **comedy** of mistaken identifies and subterfuge more romantic than the original. In *I Supposti* the Bianca character has already been seduced; and her seducer is seeking a wife with a handsome fortune: he does not fall in love at first sight. These are typical features of classical comedy, which was more **farcical** than the comedy Shakespeare wrote. Shakespeare complicates the plot by introducing more suitors and disguises than feature in the source play, adding to the theatrical appeal of *The Shrew*.

In *I Supposti* the heroine has no sister. The character of the shrew Katherina is introduced to provide a point of contrast; her wooing and wedding are to be very different from Bianca's. Shrew-taming stories were part of folklore; there were **ballads** and folk-tales dealing with the subject, and a number of literary antecedents too, in the form of early Tudor plays and poems. It is possible that Shakespeare's play was inspired by an English comedy, *The Taming of A Shrew*, which resembles *The Shrew* in a number of ways (see Critical History for references to books you can refer to if you wish to read discussions about *The Taming of A Shrew*). But Petruchio's wife-taming methods are unique in the literature of this period; he does not beat or trick his wife. What is most remarkable is the fact that Shakespeare manages to marry his two plots, from very different literary traditions, and interweave them into a cohesive whole. He manages this by focusing on the same themes in both plots (money, marriage, men and women), encouraging us to compare the characters' experiences. As *The Shrew* progresses plot and subplot become more and more closely linked, culminating in a scene where all the characters are on stage together (as they are at the wedding ceremony, although III.2 is solely concerned with Kate and Petruchio). Leading up to V.2, Shakespeare moves between his two wooing plots, focusing on one sister and then the other. Hortensio provides a neat link between the two strands of the story: he begins as a suitor in the subplot, but is then a witness to Petruchio's taming methods in Act IV. Hortensio is also suitor to a third female, the Widow. Shakespeare introduces this 'plot' to provide another point of contrast with the other couples on stage.

The differences in mood and sentiment in the alternating scenes are effective. In the taming plot there are more examples of verbal and physical violence, although the subplot includes moments of visual comedy too, centring on the use of disguises. The subplot is driven by intrigue and improvisation, while the taming plot proceeds in a more direct way: we know what Petruchio intends from I.2 onwards because he is open about his plans. It is possible to argue that the main plot has more theatrical power because it focuses on the conflict between two individuals, while there are a number of characters jostling for position in the subplot. Both plots, however, involve a degree of suspense. Will

Lucentio and Tranio get away with their disguises? Will Petruchio tame his wife? The two plots are driven by conflict and competition. In both the servants play supporting roles, helping their masters with their plans. It is **ironic** that plot and subplot, for all the mirroring that occurs, ultimately lead in different directions. The taming plot culminates in the revelation of marital peace and harmony, while the subplot, which seems more romantic, ends in discord. Realism is pitted against romanticism, and wins.

Although the play centres on the wooing of Bianca to begin with, Petruchio becomes the dramatic focus when he appears in the second scene. It can be argued that the whole play is driven by Petruchio, structured around his progress and the ways in which the other characters respond to him. Petruchio is the only character who is given **soliloquies** and he dominates both verbally and physically, mirroring the role the Lord played in the **Induction**. Repetition is a key feature of the taming plot. In each phase a pattern is repeated; Petruchio makes a decision about what he wants and then sets about achieving his aims in a very single-minded way. He wants to woo Katherina, he woos her. He decides when he will marry her; he marries her. He decides to tame her at home; he carries her off and breaks her will. Finally, Petruchio returns to Padua to prove he has tamed his wife and she demonstrates his success. As Brian Morris suggests in his introduction to the Arden edition of the play, this is a pattern of taming, teaching and testing, and suggests forward movement. In each phase, until the final one, there is an argument between hero and heroine; Kate comes off worse each time, so we know how the plot will be resolved. Other characters are used to demonstrate Petruchio's ability to dominate; he conquers Grumio, Baptista, his servants, the tailor and finally the whole gathering at the wedding feast in Act V when he wins his wager. Descriptions of events off stage add to his power and make us eager to see Petruchio in action. Throughout the play, characters in the subplot comment on the action of the main plot, further adding to its impact. There is one other feature of the structuring of the play that adds to Petruchio's power as a theatrical creation. Three key scenes, always 'highlights' on stage, focus on the fortune-hunter; the first meeting of Kate and Petruchio, the wedding ceremony and the final feast. The scene with the tailor might be added to this list. It is clear from this list that social ceremonies and rituals are an important part of the structure of *The Shrew*.

How does the Induction fit into the structure? The two main plots run parallel to one another, along lines set up by the frame. Here we see a plan outlined in one scene and carried out in the second, foreshadowing both plot and subplot. Themes are established in the Induction: illusion and transformation can be added to the list offered above. There is a tension between romance and reality; the tinker Sly is contrasted with a well-educated Lord. Most importantly, we have an introduction to the use of deception and disguises. The Induction is an ironic foreshadowing of the main action; most significantly in the transformation of Sly into a Lord. This introduces us to the idea of Kate being tamed. This Induction is the only frame of its kind in Shakespeare's work, and it too has literary antecedents; for example, the tale of a beggar who is transformed into a prince in *The Arabian Nights*. The Warwickshire drunkard is a unique theatrical creation, however. Some critics have argued that the self-conscious theatricality of the Induction (the drawing of attention to the boy actor playing Bartholomew and the players who provide the entertainment, as well as the brief comments by Sly at the end of I.1) indicates that Shakespeare wishes to undermine the validity of the wife-taming that occurs: is *everything* we see an illusion? Are *all* the characters impostors? Critics continue to discuss whether or not there was an **epilogue** (a final framing scene) that has been lost. Some directors feel that the Induction does not serve a useful purpose. Often it is dispensed with when the play is performed. But without the Induction we have a less sophisticated play, and a good deal of **dramatic irony** is lost. The frame is an important part of the whole, and Sly is an entertaining and vigorous character in his own right.

PART FOUR

TEXTUAL ANALYSIS

TEXT 1 (INDUCTION 1.1–42)

Sly is found lying outside the Inn by the Lord.

SLY: I'll feeze you, in faith.
HOSTESS: A pair of stocks, you rogue.

SLY: Y'are a baggage, the Slys are no rogues. Look in the
Chronicles, we came in with Richard Conqueror.
Therefore *paucas pallabris*, let the world slide. Sessa! 5

HOSTESS:. You will not pay for the glasses you have burst?

SLY: No, not a denier. Go by, Saint Jeronimy, go to thy
cold bed and warm thee.

HOSTESS: I know my remedy, I must go fetch the third-
borough. [*Exit*] 10

SLY: Third, or fourth, or fifth borough, I'll answer him
by law. I'll not budge an inch, boy. Let him come,
and kindly. *Falls asleep.*

Wind horns. Enter a LORD *from hunting, with his* TRAIN.

LORD: Huntsman, I charge thee, tender well my hounds.
Breathe Merriman, the poor cur is emboss'd, 15
And couple Clowder with the deep-mouth'd brach.
Saw'st thou not, boy, how Silver made it good
At the hedge corner, in the coldest fault?
I would not lose the dog for twenty pound.

FIRST HUNTSMAN: Why, Belman is as good as he, my lord. 20
He cried upon it at the merest loss,
And twice today pick'd out the dullest scent.
Trust me, I take him for the better dog.

LORD: Thou art a fool. If Echo were as fleet,
I would esteem him worth a dozen such. 25

But sup them well, and look unto them all.
Tomorrow I intend to hunt again.

FIRST HUNTSMAN: I will, my lord.

LORD: What's here? One dead, or drunk? See, doth he
breathe?

SECOND HUNTSMAN: He breathes, my lord. Were he not warm'd with ale,
This were a bed but cold to sleep so soundly. 31

LORD: O monstrous beast, how like a swine he lies!
Grim death, how foul and loathsome is thine image!
Sirs, I will practise on this drunken man.
What think you, if he were convey'd to bed, 35
Wrapp'd in sweet clothes, rings put upon his fingers,
A most delicious banquet by his bed,
And brave attendants near him when he wakes,
Would not the beggar then forget himself?

FIRST HUNTSMAN: Believe me, lord, I think he cannot choose. 40

SECOND HUNTSMAN: It would seem strange unto him when he wak'd.

LORD: Even as a flatt'ring dream or worthless fancy.

The opening of the **Induction** serves as an **ironic** commentary on the action of the play that follows it and foreshadows events and themes that will become important in both plot and subplot. The exchange between Sly and the Hostess, which concerns the drunkard's refusal to accept responsibility for his behaviour and pay for the glasses he has broken, anticipates the verbal sparring of Katherina and Petruchio, and hints at the heroine's waywardness. Sly's defiance and determination to stand up for himself mirror Kate's, but she is as powerless socially as her counterpart in the Induction. Sly is the lowest of the low, a 'beggar', just as Kate, as a woman, is considered worthless when she is a scold. The 'foulsome image' the tinker presents reflects the fact that sharp-tongued Katherina is abhorred as a 'fiend of hell' (I.1.88): both project repugnant **images**. It is clear that Sly – like Katherina – will be acted upon by more powerful men: either the law ('the third-borough') or the Lord's tricks will ensnare him. We might compare the public humiliation of the stocks that the Hostess threatens Sly with, with the public punishment that is dealt out to Katherina during her taming. Neither Sly nor Katherina are allowed to exercise their own wills; as the huntsman points out, Sly 'cannot choose': neither can Kate. She is married off and tamed against her liking.

Sly will be made to believe that he is a lord. The language used to describe the process – 'flatt'ring dream', 'worthless fancy' – suggests the magical transformation that will take place. This is exactly what occurs in the main plot, in which the other characters see the heroine's metamorphosis into an obedient wife as a 'wonder' (V.2.190). Kate is bewildered as if in a dream during her taming. Some would argue that because the Lord's trick on Sly is described as a 'fancy' we can view Petruchio's taming of Kate as a male wish-fulfilment fantasy: it is just as unexpected and preposterous. In the Induction it seems that Sly's transformation is to be a source of entertainment: but in the main plot Petruchio is in deadly earnest. Disturbing as it may seem, it is possible to view the reactions of the other characters to Katherina's humiliation at the wedding ceremony as proof that the pugilistic hero is providing his Paduan audience with a comic interlude: Gremio says, 'Went they not quickly, I should die laughing' (III.2.239). This amusement is foreshadowed later in this scene of the Induction when the Lord says that he will remain on hand to ensure that the hilarity caused by his tricks does not become too great. The Lord's delineation of Sly as barely human – he is a 'monstrous beast' – reflects the fact that the male characters all view Katherina as an inhuman devil when she exercises her tongue. Is the playwright suggesting it is legitimate to treat these inferior creatures as objects of ridicule to be used in sport? It is intriguing, and perhaps ironic, that Sly will be subjected to an onslaught of elegance and riches in his 'dream'; this is the opposite of the treatment that Kate will endure. The rogue tinker is to be made to accept his transformation through the demonstration of excessive kindness, Kate the scold through deprivation.

Sly's confused concern for his social status (his family arrived with 'Richard Conqueror') reflects the social concerns of the play. Kate is worried that she will be publicly humiliated by her family and her husband, shown by her angry words in Acts I–III, and then by her dismay when the tailor is dismissed in Act IV. Petruchio will subvert society's codes in order to force his wife to conform, and he uses his masculine power to achieve his ends. The Lord is involving himself in a reversal of the social order for the same reason. We are introduced to ideas about male linguistic power in this extract. The difference between Sly's colloquial speech ('I'll feeze thee!') and the Lord and huntsmen's more elegant style is amusing, and we immediately see who will dominate. Petruchio's forceful verbal style will similarly overrule Kate's shrewish persona; like Sly asleep, Katherina is largely silent as she is tamed.

The references to hunting and the treatment that the dogs, described in this extract, are to receive are ironic. More care is lavished on these beasts than is meted out to tinkers and women like Kate; we might argue that this is because the dogs perform a valuable service to their owner and heighten his reputation. When she submits to her husband's authority Kate is given the praise that Echo, Merriman and the rest have deserved for their efforts during the hunt. The hunting **motif** runs through *The Shrew*, clearly linking Petruchio with the Lord; both are the superior and controlling males in the scenes in which they appear. Petruchio takes on the shrew, which makes a 'little din' (I.2.198) and turns her from a 'haggard' (IV.1.180) into a tame falcon, who will perform so as to add to his prestige. The coupling of Clowder with the 'deep mouth'd brach' perhaps hints at the couplings we will see later in the play. Pairing him off is to be an important part of the Lord's scheme for deceiving Sly: in the next scene he will be presented with a 'wife'. The exhaustion of the 'emboss'd' dog mentioned at line 15 foreshadows the weary state Katherina will find herself in during her taming. Sly is linked to the animal world when he is compared to a 'swine'; animal imagery will continue to suggest the natural order of things in this play, in which unattractive animals are brought into line. The competitive discussion of the dogs' different merits foreshadows the tussle for Bianca's hand in marriage, and the comparison that will be made between the three wives who grace the table in the final scene. There is a clear indication that there is a natural order in this scene. We will not be able to escape the conclusion that women are meant to be like tame dogs and falcons, part of their husband's goods and chattels, for men to train and enjoy as and when they please. The Lord intends to go hunting again 'tomorrow'; Petruchio will expect his Kate to speak and perform on cue too.

We might feel that the **slapstick** and verbal comedy that are notable features of *The Shrew*, are established here. The joke that the

Lord sets up will involve visual comedy, and Sly's drunken slumber is comic. The incongruity of the elegant language used to describe the dogs and the more direct and pithy exclamations of and about Sly, prepare us for the wit and linguistic ingenuity that we will come to associate with Petruchio and Tranio in particular. The theme of deception, the importance of appearances and the power of transformation are also established here. Complex layers of theatrical illusion are hinted at: we suspect that Sly will be given new clothes as well as a feast when he wakes up, anticipating the use of disguises in the subplot. Are we to understand that the roles people play are a construction? Sly is to be given a false identity by the Lord, just as the women in *The Shrew* are defined by men. The important role clothes are to play in the taming plot is hinted at when we learn that Sly is to be attended by 'brave' servants (in fine array). When she fits in with the plans that have been made for her Kate will be rewarded with a new dress. Like the Lord, Petruchio will be able to choose the clothes that he and his wife wear, proving where the power lies. Finally, just as Petruchio will give Kate no time to think about what is happening to her, the Lord makes a lightning decision to play a trick on Sly. When the drunkard wakes up in the next scene he is immediately bombarded with new sensations.

TEXT 2 (III.2.189–231)

Petruchio prepares to return home with his bride after the wedding ceremony.

> PETRUCHIO: … If you knew my business,
> You would entreat me rather go than stay. 190
> And honest company, I thank you all
> That have beheld me give away myself
> To this most patient, sweet, and virtuous wife.
> Dine with my father, drink a health to me,
> For I must hence, and farewell to you all. 195
>
> TRANIO: Let us entreat you stay till after dinner.
>
> PETRUCHIO: It may not be.

GREMIO: Let me entreat you.

PETRUCHIO: It cannot be.

KATHERINA: Let me entreat you.

PETRUCHIO: I am content.

KATHERINA: Are you content to stay?

PETRUCHIO: I am content you shall entreat me stay; 200
But yet not stay, entreat me how you can.

KATHERINA: Now if you love me, stay.

PETRUCHIO: Grumio, my horse.

GRUMIO: Ay, sir, they be ready; the oats have eaten the horses.

KATHERINA: Nay then, 205
Do what thou canst, I will not go today,
No, nor tomorrow, not till I please myself.
The door is open, sir, there lies your way,
You may be jogging whiles your boots are green.
For me, I'll not be gone till I please myself. 210
'Tis like you'll prove a jolly surly groom,
That take it on you at the first so roundly.

PETRUCHIO: O Kate, content thee, prithee be not angry.

KATHERINA: I will be angry; what hast thou to do?
Father, be quiet; he shall stay my leisure. 215

GREMIO: Ay, marry, sir, now it begins to work.

KATHERINA: Gentlemen, forward to the bridal dinner.
I see a woman may be made a fool
If she had not a spirit to resist.

PETRUCHIO: They shall go forward, Kate, at thy command. 220
Obey the bride, you that attend on her.
Go to the feast, revel and domineer,
Carouse full measure to her maidenhead,

Be mad and merry, or go hang yourselves.
But for my bonny Kate, she must with me. 225
Nay, look not big, nor stamp, nor stare, nor fret;
I will be master of what is mine own.
She is my goods, my chattels, she is my house,
My household stuff, my field, my barn,
My horse, my ox, my ass, my any thing, 230
And here she stands. Touch her whoever dare!

From the courtship onwards Petruchio has been in control of events, and this extract confirms his authority. He refuses to stay for the wedding feast, in spite of entreaties from Tranio and Gremio. His repeated denial becomes more forceful (from 'It may not be' to 'It cannot be'), and then when his wife makes the same request, his answer is indirect. He forces Katherina to question him so that he can put her in her place. We might feel he is reminding her that she must get used to the idea of asking for his consent and approval ('I am content you shall entreat me stay'). The repetition of the word 'entreat' suggests that Katherina will become accustomed to verbal submission. This does not come as a surprise. The opening of this extract hints that the wife-taming has begun in earnest now; perhaps this is the 'business' Petruchio refers to at line 189. It is rather chilling that Petruchio believes that the Paduans would 'entreat me rather go than stay' if they knew what his intentions were. Are his methods to be too shocking or unpleasant to witness? It is significant that Petruchio's reference to his 'business' is immediately followed by a description of his 'most patient, sweet, and virtuous wife'. We might feel that these lines are a reproach to Kate, who clearly possesses none of these qualities in this scene. This description is also a declaration of intent: she will be forced to assume these qualities. The final lines of the extract suggest that Petruchio has the power to make this happen, since he is now Katherina's owner, she part of his 'household stuff'. Throughout this scene, Petruchio speaks with complete authority, indicated by his use of commands in the final speech ('Obey the bride … Go to the feast … Carouse full measure … go hang yourselves') culminating in a forceful statement, 'she must with me'. The modal verbs Shakespeare puts in the protagonist's mouth have become increasingly purposeful: 'must' allows no contradiction. This is entirely in keeping with the way in which

Petruchio has been portrayed so far. He remains determined, single-minded and assured.

Petruchio's behaviour retains some of the boisterous high spirits and playfulness we have come to associate with him too. He is verbally dextrous, quibbling with the Paduans and his wife, and asserting his own seemingly fantastic reality. His audience are more or less silenced by his lively final speech, and can only watch as the groom carries away his reluctant and outraged bride, pretending that she has been beset by thieves ('Touch her whoever dare!'). Petruchio continues to play the role of 'mad-brain rudesby' (II.2.10), although he is perhaps more serious here than his garb and behaviour in the church, as reported by Gremio, suggested earlier in the scene. Why is he acting out the role of subversive? Why won't he stay for the feast? Essentially, Petruchio has made a farce of his wedding because he wishes to show his wife that she must conform; or continue to suffer humiliations like those she experiences in this scene. He is attempting to alert Kate to the social chaos her shrewish behaviour leads to, and he is trying to shame her into submission by being even more perverse than she is. By being more shrew than she, Petruchio clearly shows his wife that it is useless to resist the authority of the dominant male. He can and will shout louder and longer. His refusal to stay for the feast is an example of his taming techniques; a punishment because Kate won't conform. Until she behaves in the way society expects an obedient female to behave, she will not be allowed to participate in its rituals. When she does conform Katherina will be allowed to celebrate and eat. As yet, Petruchio does not feel there is anything to be jubilant about; his wife still insists she will 'please myself'. Petruchio continues to deny her food in Act IV, when he has her at home. The reference to her 'maidenhead' hints at what will occur. Petruchio will not consummate his marriage until his wife has submitted to him publicly in Act V. By making a mockery of the celebrations that have been set up Petruchio undermines Katherina, but not himself. He gets precisely what he wants in this extract.

We might feel that Petruchio ridicules the Paduans too; the idea that they will leave to 'revel and domineer' without the bride and groom suggests that he has, in a strange way, got the better of them. In spite of Gremio's belief that 'now it begins to work', Petruchio will have the last laugh and dispel all doubts that he will not be able to master his wife. The

Paduans may feel the joke is on him (he has a shrew for a wife and Gremio's line suggests that they have a voyeuristic pleasure in seeing how the Punch and Judy show will turn out), but the audience suspects they misjudge the situation. Those who laugh at Katherina now for being 'madly mated' (III.2.242) will be made uncomfortable by the revelation that the supposedly docile Widow and Bianca are in fact shrews. Petruchio, who makes use of illusions and role-play, proves that he is the only character on stage with true understanding, or rather, he is the only character in this play forceful enough to create his own reality.

But what of the shrew herself? In this extract she delivers her last truly energetic and indignant speech about wishing to please herself, although she will try to assert her point of view when the tailor visits in Act IV. We know that there is a good deal of work to be done to bring Katherina into line when she says 'Do what thou canst, I will not go today'. Kate also pours scorn on her 'jolly surly groom', echoing her words in the earlier courting scene. But we know that she will not prevail, in spite of the fact that she can still silence some men (her father). Kate uses the same forceful modal verbs as her husband 'I *will* be angry ... He *shall* stay my leisure' – but the fact that she is ignored at line 202 suggests that the female voice has little power. There is a hint that the heroine is already being worn down and perhaps already accepts that she wants to conform. Her uncertain question, 'Are you content to stay?' suggests this, as does her next line, 'Now if you love me, stay'. This request might be a challenge, but because Kate was so worried about being jilted at the altar at the beginning of the scene, and because she is also clearly concerned about not being allowed to participate in the public triumph of her own bridal feast, we might sense that she will submit. The only – preposterous – power she is allowed in this scene is to tell the guests to go forward to the wedding feast, a command which is hijacked by her husband and revealed as an absurdity. Petruchio's pretended gallantry at this point ('They shall go forward, Kate, at thy command') further undermines her, as the description of her supposed virtues did earlier. Her stamping, staring and fretting make her seem ridiculous too. Kate may 'look ... big', but she doesn't have the verbal power to achieve anything.

The reference to Petruchio's horse is important, part of the pattern of animal **imagery** that informs our understanding of the play. This reference hints at what will occur on the journey home, when Kate comes off her horse in the mire; a visual **symbol** of her ultimate submission. Earlier in the play Katherina referred to her wooer as a 'jade' (a worn out, useless horse, II.1.201), and he invited her to 'sit on' him (II.1.198); when she falls under her horse we know Petruchio will win. This extract suggests that it is Kate and not Petruchio who is the real 'jade': she is no use to her master because she remains stormy and defiant. Petruchio's reference to his horse also reminds us of his arrival at the wedding on a broken-down horse suffering from every possible ailment (III.2.46–61). This entertaining description of the decrepit beast is a **metaphor** for Kate the useless wife, and Petruchio's arrival on it an insult to her dignity. We will see many more examples of the protagonist's perverse eccentricity in the next Act.

TEXT 3 (V.2.117–48)

The men bet on the obedience of their wives, and Katherina scolds her sister and the Widow for their froward behaviour.

PETRUCHIO: Nay, I will win my wager better yet,
And show more sign of her obedience,
Her new-built virtue and obedience.

Enter KATHERINA, BIANCA, *and* WIDOW.
See where she comes, and brings your froward wives 120
As prisoners to her womanly persuasion.
Katherine, that cap of yours becomes you not.
Off with that bauble, throw it under foot. [*She obeys.*]

WIDOW: Lord, let me never have a cause to sigh
Till I be brought to such a silly pass. 125

BIANCA: Fie, what foolish duty call you this?

LUCENTIO: I would your duty were as foolish too.
The wisdom of your duty, fair Bianca,
Hath cost me a hundred crowns since supper-time.

BIANCA: The more fool you for laying on my duty. 130

PETRUCHIO: Katherine, I charge thee, tell these headstrong women
What duty they do owe their lords and husbands.

WIDOW: Come, come, you're mocking. We will have no telling.

PETRUCHIO: Come on, I say, and first begin with her.

WIDOW: She shall not. 135

PETRUCHIO: I say she shall. And first begin with her.

KATHERINA: Fie, fie! Unknit that threatening unkind brow,
And dart not scornful glances from those eyes,
To wound thy lord, thy king, thy governor.
It blots thy beauty as frosts do bite the meads, 140
Confounds thy fame as whirlwinds shake fair buds,
And in no sense is meet or amiable.
A woman mov'd is like a fountain troubled,
Muddy, ill-seeming, thick, bereft of beauty,
And while it is so, none so dry or thirsty 145
Will deign to sip or touch one drop of it.
Thy husband is thy lord, thy life, thy keeper,
Thy head, thy sovereign …

These lines provide closure of a kind, but also raise questions. On the surface it seems that Petruchio has won 'peace … and love, and quiet life, / An awful rule and right supremacy' (V.2.109–10), and, significantly, his wager. Love, marriage and women are linked once again to money and Petruchio's supremacy over the others in all these fields is demonstrated visually and orally. Firstly, having come when she was called for, Kate throws her cap under her foot as a token of obedience. She then obeys Petruchio's command to lecture the other women on the 'duty they do owe their lords and husbands', speaking in a style and tone that reflect many of Petruchio's earlier speeches, both in content and construction. The comparison that Katherina makes between an unruly woman and a muddy fountain, which no-one will 'deign to sip', can be linked to the way food was withheld during the taming scenes. Kate can eat now because she is a good wife; she is her husband's 'super-dainty Kate'. Her listing of 'thy lord, thy life …' recalls earlier speeches made by Petruchio too, most notably his defiant description of Katherina as part of his 'household stuff' in Act III. Has she been so cowed that she now takes on her husband's voice? Or are we to assume that this couple are well-matched because she has learned to speak his language? Kate's rhetorical skill reflects Petruchio's verbal mastery of events, suggesting that he has prevailed completely. It is significant that Katherina does not speak until she is requested to. Her scolding of Bianca and the Widow, 'Fie, fie! Unknit that threatening brow' recalls his commands to her, which she has now learned to obey. And Petruchio does not simply get his wife to show her obedience and use her 'womanly persuasion' to put down the other women; he shows that he is still in control verbally. He silences the Widow with these forceful words: 'I say she shall.' It seems that Petruchio maintains his taming ability, even when his own wife is tamed; now he has so much power he can even get his wife to 'tame' the others: she carries on the war against shrews for him. A number of critics suggest that Kate's speech silences the other women in this scene. Because Petruchio has won an enormous amount of money during the play for taming Kate, we have to see him as the real winner here. And his confidence and continued domineering behaviour suggest he is well pleased with his work: he is keen for his wife to speak and show off *his* skill.

However, many critics have claimed that Katherina's speech and behaviour must be read as an **ironic** deconstruction of the patriarchy she seems to be endorsing. As Bianca says, it is ridiculous to throw off a cap and put in under a husband's foot: does this 'foolish duty' undermine Petruchio's triumph? Equally, Katherina's speech can seem exaggerated and rather ridiculous; the war **imagery** she utilises ('dart not … thine eye. … wound') which is carried on through the rest of the speech might be seen as a deliberate absurdity. The same might be said for her rhetorical listing; is she parodying Petruchio in order to suggest that *she* has in fact triumphed? When she speaks with his voice perhaps she defeats the Paduans, who have not had a good word to say for her. And how can we be sure that the 'brawling scold' of the early scenes has gone for ever, particularly when two other shrews unmask themselves? The scorn and defiance that the Widow and Bianca display here mirror Kate's early defiance, suggesting that a woman may 'break out' at any time. Really, perhaps there is no choice: all women are shrews. Hortensio's silence and Lucentio's peevish and impotent comments suggest that there is a perceptible loss of male power in this scene.

Nevertheless, it remains possible to argue that this extract proves that a happy marriage depends upon female submission. We know that two out of three couples are in for a rough ride, and the fact that Petruchio seems well pleased with what occurs ('Why there's a wench …') endorses the view of those who would argue that this final scene cannot be read ironically, for all the questions it raises. Here, women are reduced to sport when the men bet on their obedience; marriage remains a game for *men* to win or lose. The fact that money is linked to love and marriage again here suggests that the patriarchal hierarchy remains in place. Men control the money, and the most successful man gets the largest share, because he has been most successful in the terms of the world of the play, in which matrimonial bargaining has been repeatedly linked to mercantile bartering. Petruchio's goods and chattels are worth most. And the masculine competition and sporting of the wager suggests that it has all been a game, undermining the seriousness of the whole business of marriage.

Part five

Background

William Shakespeare's life

There are no personal records of Shakespeare's life. Official documents and occasional references to him by contemporary dramatists enable us to draw the main outline of his public life, but his private life remains hidden. What we do know can be quickly summarised. Shakespeare was born into a well-to-do family in the market town of Stratford-upon-Avon in Warwickshire, where he was baptised, in Holy Trinity Church, on 26 April 1564. His father, John Shakespeare, was a prosperous glover and leather merchant who became a person of some importance in the town: in 1565 he was elected an alderman of the town, and in 1568 he became high bailiff (or mayor) of Stratford. In 1557 he had married Mary Arden. Their third child (of eight) and eldest son, William, learned to read and write at the primary (or 'petty') school in Stratford and then, it seems probable, attended the local grammar school, where he would have studied Latin, history, logic and rhetoric. In November 1582 William, then aged eighteen, married Anne Hathaway, who was twenty-six years old. They had a daughter, Susanna, in May 1583, and twins, Hamnet and Judith, in 1585.

Shakespeare next appears in the historical record in 1592 when he was mentioned as a London actor and playwright in a pamphlet by the dramatist Robert Greene. These 'lost years' 1585–92 have been the subject of much speculation, but how they were occupied remains as much a mystery as when Shakespeare left Stratford, and why. In his pamphlet, *Greene's Groatsworth of Wit*, Greene expresses to his fellow dramatists his outrage that the 'upstart crow' Shakespeare has the impudence to believe he 'is as well able to bombast out a blank verse as the best of you'. To have aroused this hostility from a rival, Shakespeare must, by 1592, have been long enough in London to have made a name for himself as a playwright. We may conjecture that he had left Stratford in 1586 or 1587.

During the next twenty years, Shakespeare continued to live in London, regularly visiting his wife and family in Stratford. He continued to act, but his chief fame was as a dramatist. From 1594 he wrote exclusively for the Lord Chamberlain's Men, which rapidly became the leading dramatic company and from 1603 enjoyed the patronage of James I as the King's Men. His plays were extremely popular and he became a shareholder in his theatre company. He was able to buy lands around Stratford and a large house in the town, to which he retired in about 1611. He died there on 23 April 1616 and was buried in Holy Trinity Church on 25 April.

SHAKESPEARE'S DRAMATIC CAREER

Between the late 1580s and 1613 Shakespeare wrote thirty-seven plays, and contributed to some by other dramatists. For only a few plays is the date of their first performance known – but the broad outlines of Shakespeare's dramatic career have been established. He began in the late 1580s and early 1590s by rewriting earlier plays and working with plotlines inspired by the Classics. He concentrated on comedies (such as *The Comedy of Errors* and *The Taming of the Shrew*) and plays dealing with English history (such as the three parts of *Henry VI*, 1589–92), though he also tried his hand at bloodthirsty revenge tragedy (*Titus Andronicus*, 1592–3, indebted to both Ovid and Seneca). During the 1590s Shakespeare developed his expertise in these kinds of play to write comic masterpieces such as *A Midsummer Night's Dream* (1594–5) and *As You Like It* (1599–1600) and history plays such as *Henry IV* (1596–8) and *Henry V* (1598–9).

As the new century begins a new note is detectable. Plays such as *Troilus and Cressida* (1601–2) and *Measure for Measure* (1603–4), poised between comedy and tragedy, evoke complex responses. Because of their generic uncertainty and ambivalent tone such works are sometimes referred to as 'problem plays', but it is tragedy which comes to dominate the extraordinary sequence of masterpieces: *Hamlet* (1600–1), *Othello* (1602–4), *King Lear* (1605–6), *Macbeth* (1605–6) and *Antony and Cleopatra* (1606).

In the last years of his dramatic career, Shakespeare wrote a group of plays of a quite different kind. These 'romances', as they are often called, are in many ways the most remarkable of all his plays. The group comprises *Pericles* (1608), *Cymbeline* (1609–11), *The Winter's Tale*

(1610–11) and *The Tempest* (1610–11). These plays (particularly *Cymbeline*) reprise many of the situations and themes of the earlier dramas but in fantastical and exotic dramatic designs which, set in distant lands, covering large tracts of time and involving music, mime, dance and tableaux, have something of the qualities of masques and pageants. And the situations which in the tragedies had led to disaster are here resolved: the great theme is restoration and reconciliation.

The texts of shakespeare's plays

Nineteen of Shakespeare's plays were printed during his lifetime in what are called 'quartos' (books, each containing one play, and made up of sheets of paper each folded twice to make four leaves). Shakespeare, however, did not supervise their publication. When a playwright had sold a play to a dramatic company he sold his rights in it: copyright belonged to whoever had possession of an actual copy of the text, and so consequently authors had no control over what happened to their work. Hence, what found its way into print might be the author's copy, but it might be an actor's copy or prompt copy, perhaps cut or altered for performance; sometimes, actors (or even members of the audience) might publish what they could remember of the text.

In 1623 John Heminges and Henry Condell, two actors in Shakespeare's company, collected together texts of thirty-six of Shakespeare's plays (*Pericles* was omitted) and published them in a large folio (a book in which each sheet of paper is folded once in half, to give two leaves). This, the First Folio, was followed by later editions in 1632, 1663 and 1685. Despite its appearance of authority, however, the texts in the First Folio still present many difficulties, for there are printing errors and confused passages in the plays, and its texts often differ significantly from those of the earlier quartos, when these exist.

Shakespeare's texts have, then, been through a number of intermediaries. We do not have his authority for any one of his plays, and hence we cannot know exactly what it was that he wrote. Modern texts are what editors have constructed from the available evidence: they correspond to no sixteenth- or seventeenth-century editions, and to no early performance of a Shakespeare play.

Stanley Wells and Gary Taylor, the editors of the Oxford edition of *The Complete Works* (1988), point out that almost certainly the texts of Shakespeare's plays were altered in performance, and from one performance to another, so that there may never have been a single version. They note, too, that Shakespeare probably revised and rewrote some plays.

SHAKESPEARE & THE ENGLISH RENAISSANCE

Shakespeare arrived in London at the very time that the Elizabethan period was poised to become the 'golden age' of English literature. Although Elizabeth reigned as queen from 1558 to 1603, the term 'Elizabethan' is used very loosely in a literary sense to refer to the period 1580 to 1625, when the great works of the age were produced. (Sometimes the later part of this period is distinguished as 'Jacobean', referring to James I of England and VI of Scotland's reign from 1603 to 1625.) The poet Edmund Spenser heralded this new age with his pastoral poem *The Shepheardes Calender* (1579) and in his essay *An Apologie for Poetrie* (written about 1580, although not published until 1595) his friend Sir Philip Sidney championed the imaginative power of the 'speaking picture of poesy'.

Spenser and Sidney were part of that rejuvenating movement in European culture: the *Renaissance*. Meaning literally *rebirth* it denotes a revival and redirection of artistic and intellectual endeavour which began in Italy in the fourteenth century in the poetry of Petrarch. It spread gradually northwards across Europe, and is first detectable in England in the early sixteenth century in the writings of the scholar and statesman Sir Thomas More and in the poetry of Sir Thomas Wyatt and Henry Howard, Earl of Surrey. Its keynote was a curiosity in thought which challenged old assumptions and traditions.

That spirit was fuelled by the rediscovery of many Classical texts and the culture of Greece and Rome. This fostered a confidence in human reason and in human potential which, in every sphere, challenged old convictions. The discovery of America and its peoples (Columbus had sailed in 1492) demonstrated that the world was a larger and stranger place than had been thought. The cosmological speculation of

Copernicus (later confirmed by Galileo) that the sun, not the earth, was the centre of our planetary system challenged the centuries-old belief that the earth and human beings were at the centre of the cosmos. The pragmatic political philosophy of Machiavelli seemed to cut politics free from its traditional link with morality by permitting to statesmen any means which secured the desired end. And the religious movements we know collectively as the Reformation broke with the Church of Rome and set the individual conscience, not ecclesiastical authority, at the centre of the religious life. Nothing, it seemed, was beyond questioning, nothing impossible.

Shakespeare's drama is innovative and challenging in exactly the way of the Renaissance. It questions the beliefs, assumptions and politics upon which Elizabethan society was founded. And although the plays always conclude in a restoration of order and stability, many critics are inclined to argue that their imaginative energy goes into subverting, rather than reinforcing, traditional values. They would point out, for example, that Katherina's speech on wifely submission to patriarchal authority in *The Taming of the Shrew* (V.2.137–80) appears to be rendered **ironic** by the action of the play in which it occurs. Convention, audience expectation and censorship all required the *status quo* to be endorsed by the plots' conclusions, but the dramas find ways to allow alternative sentiments to be expressed. Frequently, figures of authority are undercut by some comic or parodic figure. Despairing, critical, dissident, disillusioned, unbalanced, rebellious, mocking voices are repeatedly to be heard in the plays, rejecting, resenting, defying the established order. They belong always to marginal, socially unacceptable figures, 'licensed', as it were, by their situations to say what would be unacceptable from socially privileged or responsible citizens. The question is: are such characters given these views to discredit them, or were they the only ones through whom a voice could be given to radical and dissident ideas? Is Shakespeare a conservative or a revolutionary?

Renaissance culture was intensely nationalistic. With the break-up of the internationalism of the Middle Ages the evolving nation states which still mark the map of Europe began for the first time to acquire distinctive cultural identities. There was intense rivalry among them as they sought to achieve in their own vernacular languages a culture which could equal that of Greece and Rome. Spenser's great allegorical epic poem *The Faerie Queene*, which began to appear from 1590, celebrated Elizabeth and was intended to outdo the poetic achievements of France and Italy and to stand beside works of Virgil and Homer. Shakespeare is equally preoccupied with national identity. His history plays tell an epic story which examines how modern England came into being through the conflicts of the fifteenth-century Wars of the Roses which brought the Tudors to the throne. He is fascinated, too, by the related subject of politics and the exercise of power. With the collapse of medieval feudalism and the authority of local barons, the royal court in the Renaissance came to assume a new status as the centre of power and patronage. It was here that the destiny of a country was shaped. Courts, and how to succeed in them, consequently fascinated the Renaissance; and they fascinated Shakespeare and his audience.

The nationalism of the English Renaissance was reinforced by Protestantism. Henry VIII had broken with Rome in the 1530s and in Shakespeare's time there was an independent Protestant state church. Because the Pope in Rome had excommunicated Queen Elizabeth as a heretic and relieved the English of their allegiance to the Crown, there was deep suspicion of Roman Catholics as potential traitors. This was enforced by the attempted invasion of the Spanish Armada in 1588. This was a religiously inspired crusade to overthrow Elizabeth and restore England to Roman Catholic allegiance. Roman Catholicism was hence easily identified with hostility to England. Its association with disloyalty and treachery was heightened by the Gunpowder Plot of 1605, a Roman Catholic attempt to destroy the government of England.

Shakespeare's plays are remarkably free from direct religious sentiment, but their emphases are Protestant. Young women, for example, are destined for marriage, not for convents. The central figures of the plays are frequently individuals beset by temptation, by the lure of evil – Angelo in *Measure for Measure*, Othello, Lear, Macbeth – and not only in tragedies: Falstaff is described as 'that old white-bearded Satan' (*1 Henry IV*, II.4.454). We follow their inner struggles. Shakespeare's heroes often have the preoccupation with self and the introspective tendencies associated with Protestantism: his tragic heroes are haunted by their consciences, seeking their true selves, agonising over what course of action to take as they follow what can often be understood as a kind of spiritual progress towards heaven or hell.

THE GLOBE THEATRE,

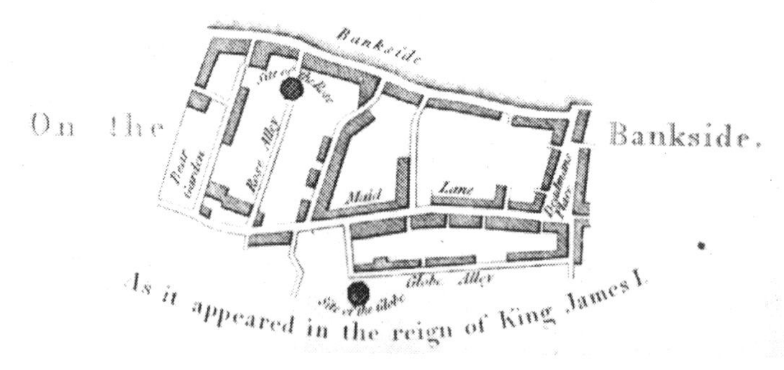

On the Bankside.

As it appeared in the reign of King James I

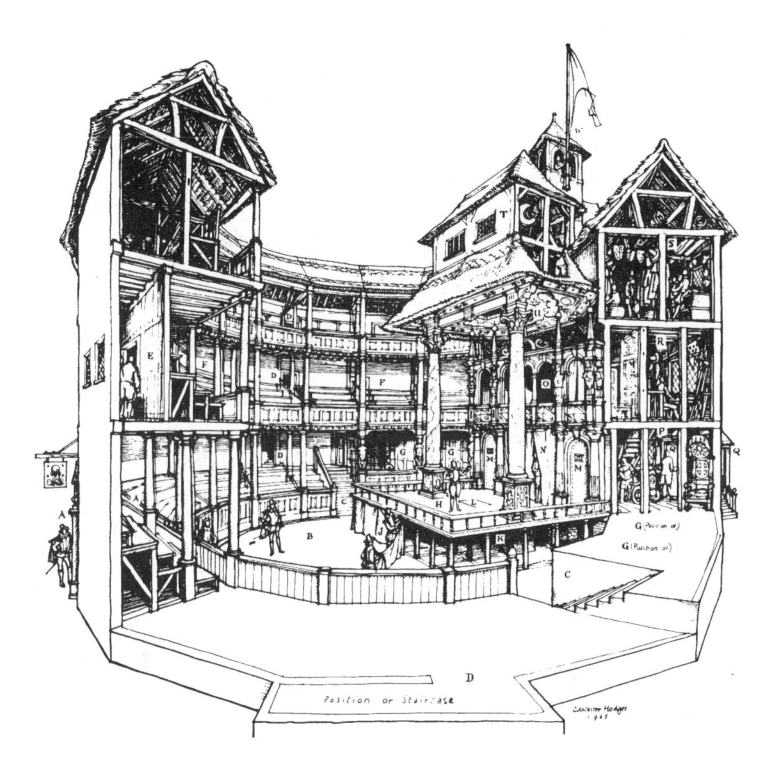

A CONJECTURAL RECONSTRUCTION OF THE INTERIOR OF THE GLOBE PLAYHOUSE

AA Main entrance
B The Yard
CC Entrances to lowest galleries
D Entrance to staircase and upper galleries
E Corridor serving the different sections of the middle gallery
F Middle gallery ('Twopenny Rooms')
G 'Gentlemen's Rooms or Lords Rooms'
H The stage
J The hanging being put up round the stage
K The 'Hell' under the stage
L The stage trap, leading down to the Hell
MM Stage doors
N Curtained 'place behind the stage'
O Gallery above the stage, used as required sometimes by musicians, sometimes by spectators, and often as part of the play
P Back-stage area (the tiring-house)
Q Tiring-house door
R Dressing-rooms
S Wardrobe and storage
T The hut housing the machine for lowering enthroned gods, etc., to the stage
U The 'Heavens'
W Hoisting the playhouse flag

The theatre for which the plays were written was one of the most remarkable innovations of the Renaissance. There had been no theatres or acting companies during the medieval period. Performed on carts and in open spaces at Christian festivals, plays had been almost exclusively religious. Such professional actors as there were wandered the country putting on a variety of entertainments in the yards of inns, on makeshift stages in market squares, or anywhere else suitable. They did not perform full-length plays, but mimes, juggling and comedy acts. Such actors were regarded by officialdom and polite society as little better than vagabonds and layabouts.

Just before Shakespeare went to London all this began to change. A number of young men who had been to the universities of Oxford and Cambridge came to London in the 1580s and began to write plays which made use of what they had learned about the Classical drama of ancient Greece and Rome. Plays such as John Lyly's *Alexander and Campaspe* (1584), Christopher Marlowe's *Tamburlaine the Great* (about 1587) and Thomas Kyd's *The Spanish Tragedy* (1588–9) were unlike anything that had been written in English before. They were full-length plays on secular subjects, taking their plots from history and legend, adopting many of the devices of Classical drama, and offering a range of characterisation and situation hitherto unattempted in English drama. With the exception of Lyly's prose dramas, they were in **blank verse**.

The most significant change of all, however, was that these dramatists wrote for the professional theatre. In 1576 James Burbage built the first permanent theatre in England, in Shoreditch, just beyond London's northern boundary. It was called simply 'The Theatre'. Others soon followed. Thus, when Shakespeare came to London, there was a flourishing drama, theatres and companies of actors waiting for him, such as there had never been before in England. His company performed at James Burbage's Theatre until 1596, and used the Swan and Curtain until they moved into their own new theatre, the Globe, in 1599. It was burned down in 1613 when a cannon was fired during a performance of Shakespeare's *Henry VIII*.

With the completion in 1996 of Sam Wanamaker's project to construct in London a replica of the Globe, and with productions now running there, a version of Shakespeare's theatre can be experienced at first-hand. It is very different to the usual modern experience of drama.

The form of the Elizabethan theatre derived from the inn yards and animal baiting rings in which actors had been accustomed to perform in the past. They were circular wooden buildings with a paved courtyard in the middle open to the sky. A rectangular stage jutted out into the middle of this yard. Some of the audience stood in the yard (or 'pit') to watch the play. They were thus on three sides of the stage, close up to it and on a level with it. These 'groundlings' paid only a penny to get in, but for wealthier spectators there were seats in three covered tiers or galleries between the inner and outer walls of the building, extending round most of the auditorium and overlooking the pit and the stage. Such a theatre could hold about 3,000 spectators. The yards were about 24m. in diameter and the rectangular stage approximately 12 x 9m. and 1.67m. high. Shakespeare aptly called such a theatre a 'wooden O' in the Prologue to *Henry V* (line 13).

The stage itself was partially covered by a roof or canopy which projected from the wall at the rear of the stage and was supported by two posts at the front. This protected the stage and performers from inclement weather, and to it were secured winches and other machinery for stage effects. On either side at the back of the stage was a door. These led into the dressing room (or 'tiring house') and it was by means of these doors that actors entered and left the stage. Between these doors was a small recess or alcove which was curtained off. Such a 'discovery place' served, for example, for Juliet's bedroom when in Act IV Scene 4 of *Romeo and Juliet* the Nurse went to the back of the stage and drew the curtain to find Juliet apparently dead on her bed. Above the discovery place was a balcony, used for the famous balcony scenes of *Romeo and Juliet* (II.2 and III.5). Actors (all parts in the Elizabethan theatre were taken by boys or men) had access to the area beneath the stage; from here, in the 'cellarage', would have come the voice of the ghost of Hamlet's father (*Hamlet*, II.1.150–82).

On these stages there was very little in the way of scenery or props – there was nowhere to store them nor any way to set them up, and, anyway, productions had to be transportable for performance at court or at noble houses. The stage was bare, which is why characters often tell us where they are: there was nothing on the stage to indicate location. It is also why location is so rarely topographical, and much more often **symbolic**. It suggests a dramatic mood or situation, rather than a place.

None of the plays printed in Shakespeare's lifetime marks Act or scene divisions. These have been introduced by later editors, but they should not mislead us into supposing that there was any break in Elizabethan performances such as might happen today. The staging of Elizabethan plays was continuous, with the many short 'scenes' of which Shakespeare's plays are often constructed following one after another in quick succession. We have to think of a more fluid and much faster production than we are generally used to: in the prologues to *Romeo and Juliet* (line 12) and *Henry VIII* (line 13) Shakespeare speaks of only two hours as the playing time.

In 1608 Shakespeare's company, the King's Men, acquired the Blackfriars Theatre, a smaller, rectangular indoor theatre, holding about 700 people, with seats for all the members of the audience, facilities for elaborate stage effects and, because it was enclosed, artificial lighting. It has been suggested that the plays written for this 'private' theatre differed from those written for the Globe, since, as it cost more to go to a private theatre, the audience came from a higher social stratum and demanded the more elaborate and courtly entertainment which Shakespeare's romances provide. However, the King's Men continued to play in the Globe in the summer, using Blackfriars in the winter, and it is not certain that Shakespeare's last plays were written specifically for the Blackfriars Theatre, or first performed there.

READING SHAKESPEARE

Shakespeare's plays were written for this stage, but there is also a sense in which they were written *by* this stage. The material and physical circumstances of their production in such theatres had a profound effect upon them. Unless we bear this in mind, we are likely to find them very strange, for we will read with expectations shaped by our own familiarity with modern, largely realistic, fiction and drama. If we try to read them like this, we shall find ourselves irritated by the improbabilities of Shakespeare's plot, confused by his chronology, puzzled by locations, frustrated by unanswered questions and dissatisfied by the motivation of the action. The absurd ease with which disguised persons pass through Shakespeare's plays is a case in point: why does no-one recognise people they know so well?

The reason is that in Shakespeare's theatre it was impossible to pretend that the audience was not watching a contrived performance. In a modern theatre, the audience is encouraged to forget itself as it becomes absorbed by the action on stage. The worlds of the spectators and of the actors are sharply distinguished by the lighting: in the dark auditorium the audience is passive, silent, anonymous, receptive and attentive; on the lighted stage the actors are active, vocal, demonstrative and dramatic. (The distinction is, of course, still more marked in the cinema.) There is no communication between the two worlds: for the audience to speak would be interruptive; for the actors to address the audience would be to break the illusion of the play. In the Elizabethan theatre, this distinction did not exist, and for two reasons: first, performances took place in the open air and in daylight which illuminated everyone equally; secondly, the spectators were all around the stage (and wealthier spectators actually on it), and were dressed no differently to the actors, who wore contemporary dress. In such a theatre, spectators would be as aware of each other as of the actors; they could not lose their identity in a corporate group, nor could they ever forget that they were spectators at a performance. There was no chance that they could believe 'this is really happening'.

This, then, was communal theatre, not only in the sense that it was going on in the middle of a crowd but in the sense that the crowd joined in. Elizabethan audiences had none of our deference: they did not keep quiet, or arrive on time, or remain for the whole performance. They joined in, interrupted, even getting on the stage. And plays were preceded and followed by jigs and clowning. It was all much more like our experience of a pantomime, and at a pantomime we are fully aware, and are meant to be aware, that we are watching games being played with reality. The conventions of pantomime revel in their own artificiality: the fishnet tights are to signal that the handsome prince is a woman, the Dame's monstrous false breasts signal that 'she' is a man.

Something very similar is the case with Elizabethan theatre: it utilised its very theatricality. Instead of trying to persuade spectators that they are not in a theatre watching a performance, Elizabethan plays acknowledge the presence of the audience. It is addressed not only by prologues, epilogues and choruses, but in **soliloquies**. There is no realistic reason why characters should suddenly explain themselves to empty rooms, but, of course, it is not an empty room. The actor is surrounded by people. Soliloquies are not addressed to the world of the play: they are for the audience's benefit. And that audience's complicity is assumed: disguises are taken to be impenetrable, however improbable, and we are to accept impossibly contrived situations, such as barely hidden characters remaining undetected.

These, then, are plays which are aware of themselves as dramas; in critical terminology, they are self-reflexive, commenting upon themselves as dramatic pieces and prompting the audience to think about the theatrical experience. They do this not only through their direct address to the audience but through their fondness for the play-within-a-play (which reminds the audience that the encompassing play is also a play) and their constant use of **images** from, and allusions to, the theatre. They are fascinated by role playing, by acting, appearance and reality. Things are rarely what they seem, either in **comedy** (for example, in *A Midsummer Night's Dream*) or tragedy (*Romeo and Juliet*). This offers one way to think about those disguises: they are thematic rather than realistic. In *As You Like It*, for example, Rosalind is more truly herself disguised as a man than when dressed as a woman.

The effect of all this is to confuse the distinction we would make between 'real life' and 'acting'. The case of Rosalind raises searching questions about gender roles, about how far it is 'natural' to be womanly or manly: how does the stage, on which a man can play a woman playing a man (and have a man fall in love with him/her), differ from life, in which we assume the roles we think appropriate to masculine and feminine behaviour? The same is true of political roles: when a Richard II or Lear is so aware of the regal part he is performing, of the trappings and rituals of kingship, their plays raise the uncomfortable possibility that the answer to the question, what constitutes a successful king, is simply: a good actor. Indeed, human life generally is repeatedly rendered through the imagery of the stage, from Macbeth's 'Life's but a walking shadow, a poor player / That struts and frets his hour upon the stage / And then is heard no more …' (V.5.23–5) to Prospero's paralleling of human life to a performance which, like the globe (both world and theatre) will end (IV.I.146–58). When life is a fiction, like this play, or this play is a fiction like life, what is the difference? 'All the world's a stage … ' (*As You Like It*, II.7.139).

PART SIX

CRITICAL HISTORY & BROADER PERSPECTIVES

THE PLAY IN PERFORMANCE

The Taming of the Shrew has been a popular play in performance, inspiring a number of adaptations and even a comedy sequel (John Fletcher's *The Woman's Prize, or The Tamer Tamed*, *c.*1611). Because of the difficulty of knowing whether Shakespeare's play or the anonymous *The Taming of A Shrew* (see Note on the Text) is being referred to, it is difficult to say when Shakespeare's play was first played and commented on. It seems possible that *The Shrew* was performed at St James' for the King and Queen in 1633 and was well received. Thereafter its fortunes languished until the nineteenth century. After the Restoration Grumio was elevated to the central role (Sander) in a rather brutal reworking of the play by John Lacy of 1667 (*Sauny the Scott*), and the actor David Garrick cut the text to arrive at his own extremely popular *Catherine and Petruchio*, first performed in 1754. This version of the shrew-taming story dominated the stage for almost thirty years. Brian Morris, editor of the current Arden edition of the play, argues that this adaptation and its predecessors succeeded in keeping Shakespeare's play off the stage until the middle of the nineteenth century. Garrick's adaptation was used by Frederick Reynolds for his opera of 1828, and then in 1948 another musical version of the story appeared, the enormously popular *Kiss Me Kate* by Cole Porter. It was not until 1844 that Shakespeare's text was revived on the stage, but by the end of the century it was being performed regularly. There have been a number of productions this century, and the play is now a firm favourite with audiences, in spite of the fact that a number of modern critics find its philosophy objectionable.

EARLY VIEWS

As mentioned above, it is difficult to be sure whether the early comments that survive are remarks about Shakespeare's text, or *A Shrew*. However, it is clear that Pepys found the version of the play he saw in 1667 unsatisfactory and 'silly'. Dr Johnson was more positive. He felt that 'the two plots are so well united, that they can hardly be called two, without injury to the art with which they are interwoven. The attention is entertained with all the variety of a double plot, yet is not distracted by unconnected incidents.' He found 'the part between Catharine and Petruchio ... eminently sprightly' and declared the play 'very popular and diverting'. The critic Hazlitt shared similar views, although he rejected Johnson's readings of Shakespeare elsewhere. He saw a 'downright moral' in *The Shrew* and noted the 'bustle, animation, and rapidity of action'. For him the play 'shows admirably how self-will is only to be got the better of by stronger will, and how one degree of ridiculous perversity is only to be driven out by another still greater.' At this point in history it is clear that it has not yet occurred to critics to question whether a man has a right to get the better of a woman with his 'stronger will': this idea will be taken up by twentieth-century critics.

It is noticeable that earlier critics responded favourably to Petruchio and his antics. Hazlitt continues, 'Petruchio is ... a very honest fellow ... He acts his assumed character to the life, with the most fantastical extravagance, with complete presence of mind, with untired animal spirits, and without particle of ill humour from beginning to end ... ' By the end of the nineteenth century, commentators began to question how we should respond to Petruchio and his wife-taming tricks. The playwright George Bernard Shaw was contemptuous of the adaptation that he saw on the stage in 1888, commenting in *The Pall Mall Gazette* on 8 June that, 'In spite of [Petruchio's] winks and smirks when Katherine is not looking, he cannot make the spectacle of a man cracking a whip at a starving woman otherwise than disgusting and unmanly.' Elsewhere, Shaw's comments on *The Taming of the Shrew* were contradictory. He felt that Shakespeare's comedy was 'realistic', Petruchio 'an honest and masterly picture of a real man, whose like we have all met' and the play as a whole 'quite bearable', 'because the selfishness of the man is healthily good-humoured and untainted by wanton cruelty', adding, 'it is good for the shrew to encounter a force like that and be brought to her senses'. It is hard to reconcile these remarks with his verdict on the final scene, which was, he declared, 'altogether disgusting to a modern sensibility. No man can sit it out in the company of a woman without being extremely ashamed of the lord-of-creation moral implied in the wager and the speech put into the woman's own mouth.' Shaw concluded that a producer would need 'some apology' for presenting the play. In recent years, the theatre critic Michael Billington has expressed the same view, calling the play 'totally offensive' and suggesting that it should be left on the shelf. Shaw was among the first to note that there is an incongruity between Katherina's speech in the early acts and the final scene. This idea has preoccupied a number of twentieth-century critics, who continue to be torn about whether or not the play is repugnant or legitimately entertaining and lively.

Michael Billington's comments can be found, with a selection of others, in The Cambridge School Shakespeare, *The Taming of the Shrew*, CUP, eds, Michael Fynes-Clinton and Perry Mills, Cambridge University Press, 1992

Comments by Johnson, Hazlitt and Shaw appear in the following books:

Johnson on Shakespeare, ed. Walter Raleigh, Oxford University Press, 1908 (1968)

The Romantics on Shakespeare, ed. Jonathan Bate, Penguin, 1992

Shakespeare's Comedies, an Anthology of Modern Criticism, ed. Laurence Lerner, Penguin, 1967

F.E. Halliday, *Shakespeare and his Critics*, Gerald Duckworth and Co. Ltd, 1949

TWENTIETH-CENTURY VIEWS

As we have seen, Katherina has not yet attracted much critical attention, although Petruchio's character was dwelt on. The balance has been redressed, particularly since the development of **feminist** criticism in the second half of this century. But before we consider more current observations on the play, it is worth considering what earlier twentieth-century commentators have said about *The Taming of the Shrew*.

Critics remained divided about the dramatic interest of the subplot, depending upon whether they believed Shakespeare was responsible for writing all three parts of the drama (**Induction**, plot and subplot).

Gradually, as the authorship of the text has become less contentious, the views expounded by Dr Johnson and Hazlitt have come to dominate. Most critics agree that Shakespeare has interwoven his plots and themes effectively. The network of intrigues and deceptions that we are presented with continues to delight and impress audiences and readers. Attention has been paid to the sources Shakespeare used, and the influence of Roman and Italian comedy on the construction and content of *The Shrew*. H.B. Charlton (1938) sees a 'germ of romanticism' in the play because the lovers Bianca and Lucentio mean to marry (in the source play they have enjoyed an illicit love-affair that results in pregnancy). Yet he casts doubt on Petruchio as a lover, characterising the central couple as 'dwellers in a menagerie'. Charlton feels that there is 'a brutal insistence on the animal in man' in the main plot. We are slowly moving away from the untroubled early readings of the presentation of the relationship between the sexes. Unlike Shaw, however, Charlton does not feel that Shakespeare intended us to take the message or moral of the play seriously. He argues that no Elizabethan or modern man or woman 'could really hold to the underlying assumption that marriage is mainly an economic arrangement'. Charlton's views raise questions that have continued to perplex readers and critics.

Overall, the predominant view before the 1950s was that Shakespeare's comedies were 'happy' plays. Gary Waller characterises this approach as one which saw the comedies as 'escapist crowd pleasers, golden effusions of romantic celebration and sentimentality'. Commentators concentrated on what they saw as universal themes and values: 'appearance and reality, courtship and marriage, idealism and cynicism, innocence and experience, order and disorder' (see Waller, p. 4). Critics also began to moralise about and psychologise the characters, following in the steps of A.C. Bradley, whose critical approach and methods had been influential since the beginning of the century. Critics explored the ways in which society's most important and meaningful rituals and myths were explored in Shakespeare's plays. The comedies were linked to pre-modern community festivals and rituals, or, as Leo Salingar suggests 'the ideas of holiday pastime and courtly revels'. In *The Shrew* this critic sees 'knockabout, practical jokes and disguises, of a kind appropriate to the Tudor Christmas holidays, the season of Misrule'. Salingar feels that Shakespeare is deliberately attempting to compare 'romantic love and acquired culture', noting the transformative powers of the former. But he also notes that Shakespeare treats Lucentio's romantic assumptions with **irony**: a view that has been more or less universally accepted today. Another critic writing in the 1970s, Alexander Leggatt, suggests that there is a sense of dislocation produced by the way in which Petruchio and the Lord work on their victims' minds. This critic comments on the self-consciously theatrical nature of the text, making much of the dreamlike and illusory qualities it contains. The self-consciousness of the text is a central theme in current critics' discussions of *The Shrew*.

Gary Waller, ed., *Shakespeare's Comedies*, Longman, Harlow, 1991

The introduction is extremely thorough, charting the history of approaches to Shakespeare's comedies in the twentieth century; including the approaches mentioned below in Current Views

H.B. Charlton, *Shakespearean Comedy*, Methuen, London, 1938 (1967)

Charlton looks closely at the traditions of comedy in Europe and at the models Shakespeare used while working on *The Shrew*

E.M.W. Tillyard, *Shakespeare's Early Comedies*, Athlone Press, London, 1965 (1983)

There is a useful introduction on the dramatic, narrative and anthropological range of Shakespeare's comedy; there is a sympathetic reading of Petruchio's character too

Alexander Leggatt, *Shakespeare's Comedy of Love*, Methuen, London, 1974

Leggatt looks at the clashes and contrasts of style in the play (romance-realism), and at the use of dreams

Leo Salingar, *Shakespeare and the Traditions of Comedy*, Cambridge University Press, 1974

CURRENT APPROACHES

More recently critics have redirected their approaches to Shakespeare's comedies. Now commentators are more inclined to relate them to the era in which the plays were written; they are no longer seen as possessing and expressing universal, enduring values: they are a product of a specific time, place and culture. Modern critics concentrate on gender and class issues, becoming increasingly interested in the subversive and self-consciously theatrical elements of the text. Feminist, **new historicist** and **psychoanalytic** critics have had a good deal to say about *The Shrew* and how its meanings are constructed. Contradictory readings continue to proliferate.

Feminist critics are divided about whether or not we can view the action of this play as supporting or subverting the patriarchal hierarchy that is described in Katherina's last speech. After discussing Kate's shrewish literary antecedents, Lisa Jardine argues that there is an 'entire absence of any locating tone' in the final lecture, which allows for 'conflicting and contradictory readings'. However, she feels that it is only the critic who 'imputes a celebratory tone to Kate's utterance at all'. To support her case Jardine considers the way in which the female tongue seems to signify impudence and immodesty in this play: 'the woman with the sharp tongue breaks the social order: she is distinctly disorderly … she threatens to sabotage the domestic harmony which depends upon her general submissiveness'. So, in order for harmony to be restored, Kate's chattering and scolding must cease. By way of contrast, Leah Marcus feels that it 'is by no means clear' that Katherina is 'converted' at the end of the play, in spite of the fact that there is 'a strong illusion of reality' surrounding this final speech. Marcus argues that Katherina learns to speak the 'pedagogue's language of social and familial order' thereby showing that she is a fine student of '**humanist** doctrine'. Other feminist critics have argued that we must view Kate's final speech as an **ironic** construct. These critics would suggest, as Germaine Greer has, that the heroine is lucky to meet a man who suits her so well. Many would dispute this. Jardine, in terms familiar from much feminist criticism of *The Shrew*, calls Petruchio a 'fortune-hunting rascal', marking a radical departure from the early positive descriptions of the hero by male commentators. Some feminists argue that the play is a satire on male chauvinism. Others would reject this, defining *The Shrew* as a product intended to affirm traditional views of men and women's roles. The debate about whether or not the play is sexist and/or misogynistic will doubtless continue to rage.

New historicist readings of *The Shrew* are often linked to feminist critiques, as commentators examine Elizabethan and Jacobean texts as 'articulations of the society's dominant cultural forces'. Karen Newman considers family politics in their historical context and produces a persuasive reading of the play, which concludes that the representation of gender is both 'patriarchally suspect and sexually ambivalent'. She suggests that the play clings to 'patriarchal ideology' while also 'tearing it away by foregrounding its constructed character'. She points to the use of the framing device and the presence of boy actors on the Elizabethan stage to support her views. Leah Marcus also draws attention to the Sly Induction in her arguments about the way patriarchy is presented in the play; she suggests that the drunkard's presence highlights and casts doubt on the hierarchy that is seeking to tame Kate. Joel Fineman adds to these ideas by suggesting that we become conscious of the constructed nature of speech in the play; Petruchio takes on a woman's shrewish tongue in order to beat his wife into submission; but whereas her tongue is powerless, he is 'never more patriarchal' than when he is acting the shrew. In her Penguin Critical Study of *The Shrew*, Stevie Davies is interested in class issues too. She says that the play 'reflects the blurring of class distinctions in the exchangeability of Tranio and his man'. She argues that both plots 'raise the ghost of possible revolt on the part of the servant class' (p. 79), although she does not believe the text ultimately endorses rebellion. She does, however, suggest that Petruchio's 'pathologically violent verbal and physical behaviour exposes the basis of force upon which the patriarchal system of marriage, the subordination of women and the ownership of property are founded' (p. 6). More positively, Frances E. Dolan suggests that the play explores the ways in which husband and wife have to 'negotiate' their relationship. In her view the text also shows us the 'disparity between public and private conduct' and 'the clash of ideals' in Renaissance marriage.

Psycholanalytic critics consider the 'struggle for differentiation between child and parent' that occurs in the comedies. For these commentators, the family becomes a 'site of instability … a place where often one parent is missing and where its harmonies are tentative, patched and together, founded on a utopian wish rather than reassuring coherence' (see Waller, p. 16). It is certainly possible to argue that *The Shrew* highlights these dilemmas. The Minolas are a dysfunctional family, who some might feel are 'cured' by Petruchio: he is astute enough to work out a suitable treatment for the reluctant bride. There have been attempts to account for Katherine's shrewishness using modern psychology: she is a neglected, hysterical child with an unpleasant family she needs to escape from in order to 'heal'. The ending of the play does not suggest that there is a 'reassuring coherence' to the events that we have seen. Hortensio and Lucentio are going to have to negotiate for domestic harmony with their partners; they cannot take it for granted.

J.D. Huston, *Shakespeare's Comedies of Play*, New York, 1981

Lisa Jardine, *Still Harping on Daughters*, Harvester Press, 1983

Chapter 4 focuses specifically on *The Shrew* ('Shrewd or shrewish? When the disorderly woman has her head'). Jardine looks at the historical and literary contexts closely and writes persuasively about the text

Joel Fineman, 'The turn of the shrew', in *Shakespeare and the Question of Theory*, eds, Patricia Parker and Geoffrey Hartman, Methuen, London, 1985

Fineman looks at the use of male and female discourse in the play

John C. Bean, 'Comic Structure and the Humanising of Kate in *The Taming of The Shrew*', in *The Woman's Part: Feminist Criticism of Shakespeare*, eds., Carolyn Ruth Swift Lenz, Gayle Greene, Carol Thomas Neely, University of Illinois Press, Urbana and Chicago, 1980 (1985)

Bean takes on the revisionists and antirevisionists, arguing for a **humanist** reading of the play, in which Kate 'discovers her own identity'

Karen Newman, 'Renaissance Family Politics and Shakespeare's *The Taming of the Shrew*', *English Literary Renaissance*, Vol. 16, 1968, pp. 86–100

Newman's essay can also be found in the Waller collection mentioned above

P.J. Gabriner, 'Hierarchy, Harmony and Happiness: Another Look at the Hunting Dogs in the "Induction" to *The Taming of the Shrew*', in *Reclamations of Shakespeare*, ed., A.J. Hoenlaars, DQR Studies in Literature 15, Rodopi, Amsterdam, GA, 1994

Gabriner argues that Kate is 'liberated into her true nature'

Stevie Davies, *The Taming of the Shrew*, Penguin Critical Studies, Penguin, 1995

A thorough feminist examination of all aspects of the text, including its historical context

Leah Marcus, 'The Shakespearean Editor as Shrew-Tamer', in *Shakespeare and Gender, A History*, eds., Deborah Barker and Ivo Kamps, Verso, London, 1995

Marcus focuses on the Induction, arguing that it reinforces the idea that Kate is tamed, and looks closely at *The Taming of A Shrew*, discussing the merits of this play

Frances E. Dolan, ed., *The Taming of the Shrew: Texts and Contexts*, Bedford Books of St. Martin's Press, New York, 1996

Includes the text of the play, comments on the historical context of the play, and extracts from a number of Renaissance texts on marriage, the household, shrew-taming. Extremely useful for any student wishing to view the play in relation to social, literary and historical contexts

Chronology

World events	Shakespeare's life	Literature/drama
1492 Columbus sets sail for America		
		1509 Ludovico Ariosto, *I Suppositi* (source)
		1513 Niccolo Machiavelli, *The Prince*
		1528 Castiglione's *Book of the Courtier*
1534 Henry VIII breaks with Rome		
		1554 Matteo Bandelli, *Novelle*
1556 Archbishop Cranmer burnt at stake		
		1562 Lope de Vega, great Spanish dramatist, born
	1564 (26 April) William Shakespeare baptised, Stratford-upon-Avon	
		1566 George Gascoigne, *Supposes* (source)
1570 Elizabeth I excommunicated by Pope Pius V		
	1576 James Burbage builds the first theatre in England, at Shoreditch	
1577 Francis Drake sets out on voyage round the world		
		1580 (c) Sir Philip Sydney, *An Apologie for Poetrie*
	1582 Shakespeare marries Anne Hathaway	
	1583 Their daughter Susanna born	
1584 Raleigh's sailors land in Virginia		**1584** John Lyly, *Alexander and Campaspe*
	1585 Their twins, Hamnet and Judith, born	
1587 Execution of Mary Queen of Scots		
1588 The Spanish Armada defeated		**1588-9** Thomas Kydd, *The Spanish Tragedy*
	late 1580s - early 1590s Probably writes *Henry VI, (parts I, II & III)* and *Richard III*	
		1590 Edmund Spenser, *Faerie Queene* (Books I-III)
1592 Plague in London closes theatres	**1592** Recorded as being a London actor and an 'upstart crow'	
	1592-4 Writes *The Comedy of Errors*	
	1594 onwards Writes exclusively for the Lord Chamberlain's Men	**1594** *A Pleasant Conceited Historie called The Taming of a Shrew* (authorship unknown) entered on the Stationer's Register

World events	Shakespeare's life	Literature/drama
	1595 (pre) *Two Gentlemen of Verona* and *Love's Labour's Lost* probably written	**1595** Death of William Painter, whose *Palace of Pleasure* provided sources of plots for many Elizabethan dramas
	1595 (c) *Romeo and Juliet*	
1596 English raid on Cadiz	**1596-8** First performance, *The Merchant of Venice*	
	1598-9 Globe Theatre built at Southwark; probably writes *Much Ado About Nothing*	
	1600 *A Midsummer Night's Dream, Much Ado About Nothing* and *The Merchant of Venice* printed in quartos	
	1600-1 *Hamlet*	
	1600-2 *Twelfth Night* written	
1603 Death of Queen Elizabeth Tudor; accession of James Stuart	**1603** onwards His company enjoys patronage of James I as the King's Men	
	1604 *Othello* performed	
1605 Discovery of Guy Fawkes's plot	**1605** First version of *King Lear*	**1605** Cervantes, *Don Quijote de la Mancha*
	1606 *Macbeth*	
	1606-7 *Antony and Cleopatra*	
	1608 The King's Men acquire Blackfriars Theatre for winter performances	
1609 Galileo constructs first astronomical telescope		
1610 William Harvey discovers circulation of blood	**1610** *Coriolanus* written	
	1611 *Cymbeline, The Winter's Tale* and *The Tempest* performed	
1612 Last burning of heretics in England		
	1613 Globe Theatre burns down	
	1616 Death of William Shakespeare	
1618 Raleigh executed for treason; Thirty Years War begins in Europe		
		1622 Birth of French dramatist Molière
	1623 First folio of Shakespeare's works includes ***The Taming of the Shrew***	

aside common dramatic convention, in which a character speaks in such a way that some of the characters on stage do not hear what is said, while others do. It may also be a direct address to the audience, revealing the character's inner thoughts, views, motives or intentions

ballad (Fr. 'dancing song') poem or song which tells a story in simple, colloquial language. There are traditional oral ballads, folk and literary ballads. The subject matter of ballads is usually tragic, and often violent. During the Elizabethan period ballads were accessible to a wide section of the populace; they were sung in the streets by their sellers, and mass produced. There were a number of comic ballads about shrewish wives

blank verse unrhymed iambic pentameter: a line of five iambs. One of the commonest English metres. It was introduced into England by Henry Howard, Earl of Surrey, who used it in his translation of Virgil's *Aeneid* (1557). Thereafter it became the normal medium for Elizabethan and Jacobean drama. The popularity of blank verse is due to its flexibility and relative closeness to spoken English

closure the impression of completeness and finality achieved by the ending of some works of literature

comedy (Gk. 'merry-making, comic poet') a broad genre which encompasses a large variety of different kinds of literature; however, 'comedy' is used most often with reference to a kind of drama which is intended to entertain the audience, and which ends happily for the characters. In this meaning of the word, comedy, like tragedy, is an ancient form dating at least as far back as the fifth century

commedia dell'arte (It. 'comedy of the professional actors') A form of drama that evolved in sixteenth-century Italy in which travelling companies of actors improvised comic plays around standard plots, using stock characters. A typical play might involve a young lover, the 'Inamorato', tricking Pantaleone ('Pantaloon'), a rich old father, into giving up his daughter. Arlecchino ('Harlequin'), the cunning servant, and Pulcinella ('Punch'), the hunchbacked clown, were other stock types. The play was enlivened by dancing, singing and slapstick buffoonery. Many elements of the form are visible in comic plays by Shakespeare, especially this play and *The Comedy of Errors*

dramatic irony feature of many plays: it occurs when the development of the plot allows the audience to possess more information about what is happening than some of the characters on stage. Characters may also speak or act in an ironic way, saying something that points to events to come without understanding the significance of what they say

epilogue (Gk. 'speech on') concluding speech or passage in a work of literature, often summing up and commenting on what has gone before; the epilogue may help to achieve closure

farce (Lat. 'to stuff') drama intended primarily to provoke laughter, using exaggerated characters and complicated plots, full of absurd episodes, ludicrous situations and knock-about action. Farcical episodes date back to Aristophanes and occur alongside serious drama in all ages

feminist, feminism broadly speaking, a political movement claiming political and economic equality of women with men. Feminist criticism and scholarship seek to explore the masculine 'bias' in texts and challenge traditional ideas about them, constructing and then offering a feminine perspective on works of art. Since the late 1960s feminist theories about literature and language, and feminist interpretations of texts have multiplied enormously. Feminism has its roots in previous centuries; early texts championing women's rights include Mary Wollstonecraft's *A Vindication of the Rights of Women* (1792) and J. S. Mill's *The Subjection of Women* (1869)

figurative language (Lat. 'to shape, form or conceive') any form of expression or grammar which deviates from the plainest expression of meaning is designated 'figurative language'. Departures into more decorative language are further defined by a large number of terms. Metaphor is probably the figure of speech which most clearly characterises literary language: hence 'figurative language' can specifically refer to metaphorical language as well as to language abounding in other figures of speech

humanist originally refers to a scholar of the humanities, especially Classical literature. At the time of the Renaissance European intellectuals devoted themselves to the rediscovery and intense study of first Roman and then Greek literature and culture, in particular the works of Cicero, Aristotle and Plato. Out of this period of intellectual ferment there emerged a view of man and a philosophy quite different from medieval scholasticism: in the nineteenth century this trend in renaissance thought was labelled 'humanism'. Reason, balance and a proper dignity for man were the central ideals of humanist thought. The humanists' attitude to the world is anthropocentric: instead of regarding man as a fallen, corrupt and sinful creature, their idea of truth and excellence is based on human values and human experience. They strive for moderate, achievable, even worldly aims, rather than revering asceticism

imagery, image (Lat. 'copy', 'representation') in its narrowest sense an image is a word-picture, a description of some visible scene or object. More commonly, imagery refers to the figurative language in a piece of literature (metaphors and similes); or all the words which refer to objects and qualities which appeal to the senses and feelings. Thematic imagery is imagery (in the general sense) which recurs through a work of art: for example, images of card-playing, hunting and hawking are all invoked in *The Shrew* to suggest the way in which the male characters relate to their womenfolk (see Imagery)

induction (Lat. 'leading in') an archaic word for the prologue introducing a work

irony (Gk. 'dissembling') saying one thing while you mean another. However, not all ironical statements in literature are as easily understood; the patterns of irony – of situation, character, structure and vocabulary – may need careful unravelling. Sometimes the writer will have to rely on the audience sharing values and knowledge in order for his or her meaning to be understood. Ironic literature characteristically presents a variety of possible points of view about its subject matter

metaphor (Gk. 'a carrying over') goes further than a comparison between two different things or ideas by fusing them together: one thing is described as being another thing, thus 'carrying over' all its associations

motif (O. Fr., from Lat. 'moving') some aspect of literature (a type of character, theme or image) which recurs frequently. An individual work may have its own recurring motifs, or leitmotifs, repeated phrases, images, descriptions or incidents. In *The Shrew* there are a number of repeated words, phrases and images, most frequently to do with hunting/wife-taming

new historicist, historicism the work of a loose affiliation of critics who discuss literary works in terms of their historical contexts. In particular, they seek to study literature as part of a wider cultural history, exploring the relationship of literature to society

psychoanalytic criticism Freud developed the theory of psychoanalysis as a means of curing neuroses in his patients, but its concepts were expanded by him and his followers as a means of understanding human behaviour and culture generally. Literature and creative processes always figured largely in his accounts of the human mind, as both example and inspiration: he asserted that many of his ideas had been anticipated in great literary works, and the terms he devised for his concepts (such as the Oedipus complex), illustrate his reliance on literary models. Critics who adopt a psychoanalytical approach explore the psychological conflicts in texts, seeking to uncover the latent content and psychological realities that underlie the work of art; they look at symbolism and hidden meanings

pun (possibly from It. 'fine point') a 'play on words': two widely different meanings are drawn out of a single word, usually for comic, witty or playful purposes

slapstick broad comedy with knock-about action, fighting, clowning, people falling over each other. So called after the stick carried by the Harlequin in *commedia dell'arte* which was constructed of two pieces of wood which slapped together to produce a loud crack when used in mock fights

soliloquy (Lat. 'speak alone') curious but fascinating dramatic convention, which allows a character in a play to speak directly to the audience, as if thinking aloud about motives, feelings and decisions. The psychological depth which the soliloquy gives to Shakespeare's tragedies in particular, is inestimable. Part of the convention is that the soliloquy provides accurate access to the character's innermost thoughts

stichomythia a dialogue carried out in single alternating lines

symbol something that represents something else (often an idea or quality) by analogy or association

AUTHOR OF THIS NOTE

Rebecca Warren teaches English Language and Literature at Luton Sixth Form College. She was educated at the universities of Stirling, California (Berkeley), Warwick and Leicester. She is the author of York Advanced Notes on *King Lear*, *Othello* and *The Mayor of Casterbridge*.

NOTES

York Notes Advanced (£3.99 each)

Margaret Atwood
Cat's Eye
Margaret Atwood
The Handmaid's Tale
Jane Austen
Mansfield Park
Jane Austen
Persuasion
Jane Austen
Pride and Prejudice
Alan Bennett
Talking Heads
William Blake
Songs of Innocence and of Experience
Charlotte Brontë
Jane Eyre
Emily Brontë
Wuthering Heights
Angela Carter
Nights at the Circus
Geoffrey Chaucer
The Franklin's Tale
Geoffrey Chaucer
The Miller's Prologue and Tales
Geoffrey Chaucer
Prologue To the Canterbury Tales
Geoffrey Chaucer
The Wife of Bath's Prologue and Tale
Joseph Conrad
Heart of Darkness
Charles Dickens
Great Expectations
Charles Dickens
Hard Times
Emily Dickinson
Selected Poems
John Donne
Selected Poems
Carol Ann Duffy
Selected Poems
George Eliot
Middlemarch
George Eliot
The Mill on the Floss
T.S. Eliot
Selected Poems
F. Scott Fitzgerald
The Great Gatsby
E.M. Forster
A Passage to India
Brian Friel
Translations
Thomas Hardy
The Mayor of Casterbridge
Thomas Hardy
The Return of the Native
Thomas Hardy
Selected Poems
Thomas Hardy
Tess of the d'Urbervilles
Seamus Heaney
Selected Poems from Opened Ground
Nathaniel Hawthorne
The Scarlet Letter
Kazou Ishiguru
The Remains of the Day
James Joyce
Dubliners
John Keats
Selected Poems
Christopher Marlowe
Doctor Faustus
Arthur Miller
Death of a Salesman
John Milton
Paradise Lost Books I & II
Toni Morrison
Beloved
William Shakespeare
Antony and Cleopatra
William Shakespeare
As You Like It
William Shakespeare
Hamlet
William Shakespeare
King Lear
William Shakespeare
Measure for Measure
William Shakespeare
The Merchant of Venice
William Shakespeare
A Midsummer Night's Dream
William Shakespeare
Much Ado About Nothing
William Shakespeare
Othello
William Shakespeare
Richard II
William Shakespeare
Romeo and Juliet
William Shakespeare
The Taming of the Shrew
William Shakespeare
The Tempest
William Shakespeare
The Winter's Tale
George Bernard Shaw
Saint Joan
Mary Shelley
Frankenstein
Alice Walker
The Color Purple
Oscar Wilde
The Importance of Being Earnest
Tennessee Williams
A Streetcar Named Desire
John Webster
The Duchess of Malfi
Virginia Woolf
To the Lighthouse
W.B. Yeats
Selected Poems

GCSE and equivalent levels (£3.50 each)

Maya Angelou
I Know Why the Caged Bird Sings

Jane Austen
Pride and Prejudice

Alan Ayckbourn
Absent Friends

Elizabeth Barrett Browning
Selected Poems

Robert Bolt
A Man for All Seasons

Harold Brighouse
Hobson's Choice

Charlotte Brontë
Jane Eyre

Emily Brontë
Wuthering Heights

Shelagh Delaney
A Taste of Honey

Charles Dickens
David Copperfield

Charles Dickens
Great Expectations

Charles Dickens
Hard Times

Charles Dickens
Oliver Twist

Roddy Doyle
Paddy Clarke Ha Ha Ha

George Eliot
Silas Marner

George Eliot
The Mill on the Floss

William Golding
Lord of the Flies

Oliver Goldsmith
She Stoops To Conquer

Willis Hall
The Long and the Short and the Tall

Thomas Hardy
Far from the Madding Crowd

Thomas Hardy
The Mayor of Casterbridge

Thomas Hardy
Tess of the d'Urbervilles

Thomas Hardy
The Withered Arm and other Wessex Tales

L.P. Hartley
The Go-Between

Seamus Heaney
Selected Poems

Susan Hill
I'm the King of the Castle

Barry Hines
A Kestrel for a Knave

Louise Lawrence
Children of the Dust

Harper Lee
To Kill a Mockingbird

Laurie Lee
Cider with Rosie

Arthur Miller
The Crucible

Arthur Miller
A View from the Bridge

Robert O'Brien
Z for Zachariah

Frank O'Connor
My Oedipus Complex and other stories

George Orwell
Animal Farm

J.B. Priestley
An Inspector Calls

Willy Russell
Educating Rita

Willy Russell
Our Day Out

J.D. Salinger
The Catcher in the Rye

William Shakespeare
Henry IV Part 1

William Shakespeare
Henry V

William Shakespeare
Julius Caesar

William Shakespeare
Macbeth

William Shakespeare
The Merchant of Venice

William Shakespeare
A Midsummer Night's Dream

William Shakespeare
Much Ado About Nothing

William Shakespeare
Romeo and Juliet

William Shakespeare
The Tempest

William Shakespeare
Twelfth Night

George Bernard Shaw
Pygmalion

Mary Shelley
Frankenstein

R.C. Sherriff
Journey's End

Rukshana Smith
Salt on the snow

John Steinbeck
Of Mice and Men

Robert Louis Stevenson
Dr Jekyll and Mr Hyde

Jonathan Swift
Gulliver's Travels

Robert Swindells
Daz 4 Zoe

Mildred D. Taylor
Roll of Thunder, Hear My Cry

Mark Twain
Huckleberry Finn

James Watson
Talking in Whispers

William Wordsworth
Selected Poems

A Choice of Poets

Mystery Stories of the Nineteenth Century including The Signalman

Nineteenth Century Short Stories

Poetry of the First World War

Six Women Poets